Floral Scapes and Tangled Art

Our first coloring book captures the natural beauty of flowers and shapes in the Zentangle® method of pattern drawing. Each page within is original hand drawn art by Brenda Shaver and her grandchildren, Cecilia Lee and Spencer Lee. Brenda is a Certified Zentangle Teacher™ trained by the co-founders of Zentangle, Maria Thomas and Rick Roberts.

Brenda teaches the Zentangle method of drawing to individuals and groups throughout Canada and the USA. Inspired by the therapeutic effect that Zentangle has on her students, Brenda and her grandchildren are producing a series of coloring books that offer hours of entertainment and creativity.

Enjoy our first book and post your coloring pages in our Facebook group "Coloring in Tangles with Brenda Shaver", and our websites
www.facebook.com/brendashaverartist
www.brendashaver.com

Happy coloring and please join us on our journey through the amazing world of tangling and art.

Brenda, Cecilia, and Spencer

Note - All drawings in this book are hand drawn using the method of pen to paper without digital or graphic design programs. Therefore you will find non perfect lines. The paper in the book may be best suited to pencil crayons and pens. Extra sheets are included if you wish to place paper between pages to prevent any bleed through using watercolours or markers.

The Zentangle® Method is an easy-to-learn, relaxing, and fun way to create beautiful images by drawing structured patterns. It was created by Rick Roberts and Maria Thomas. "Zentangle" is a registered trademark of Zentangle, Inc. To learn more and find a CZT ™ in your area, visit zentangle.com.

This book belongs to

_____

©Brenda Shaver

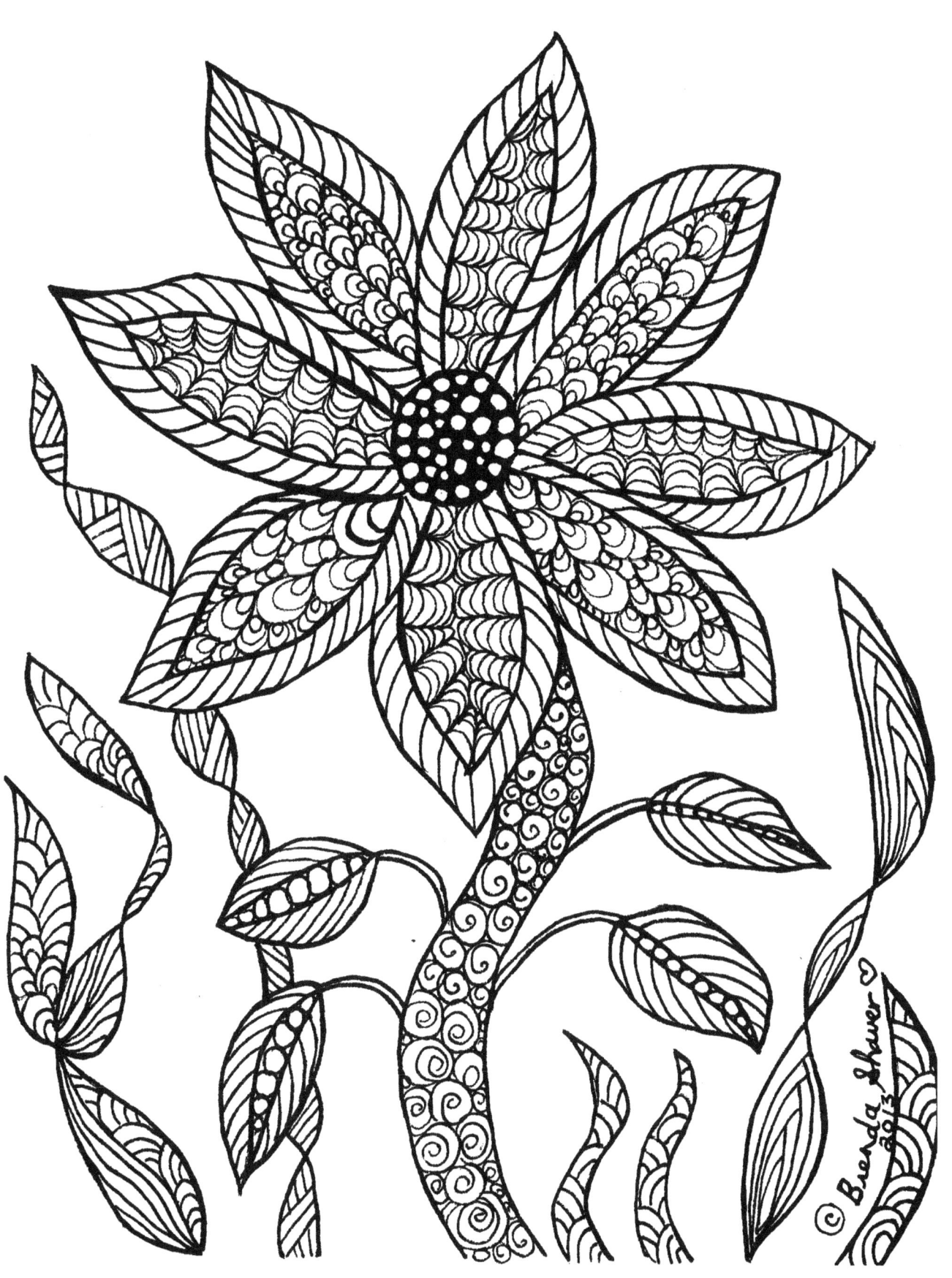

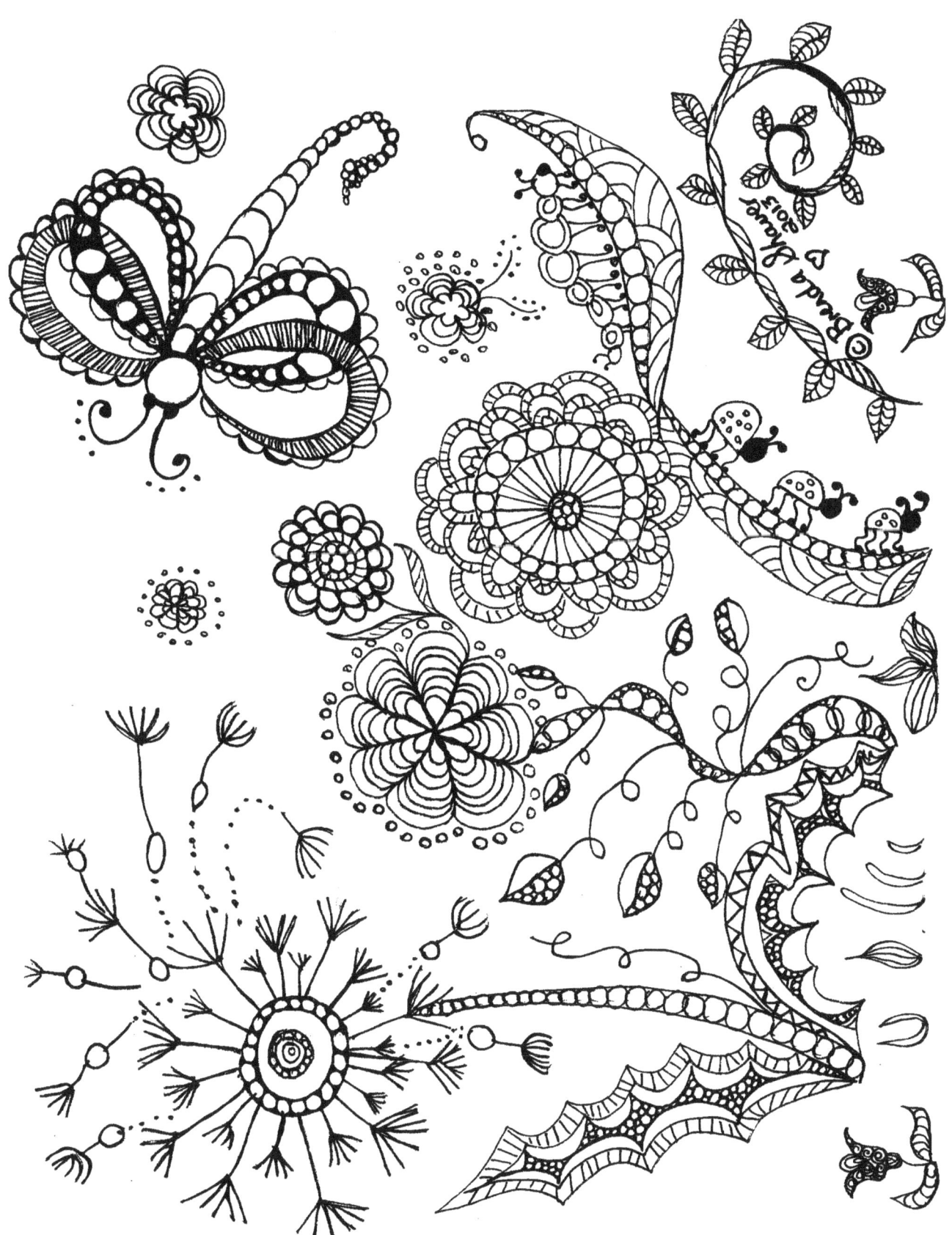

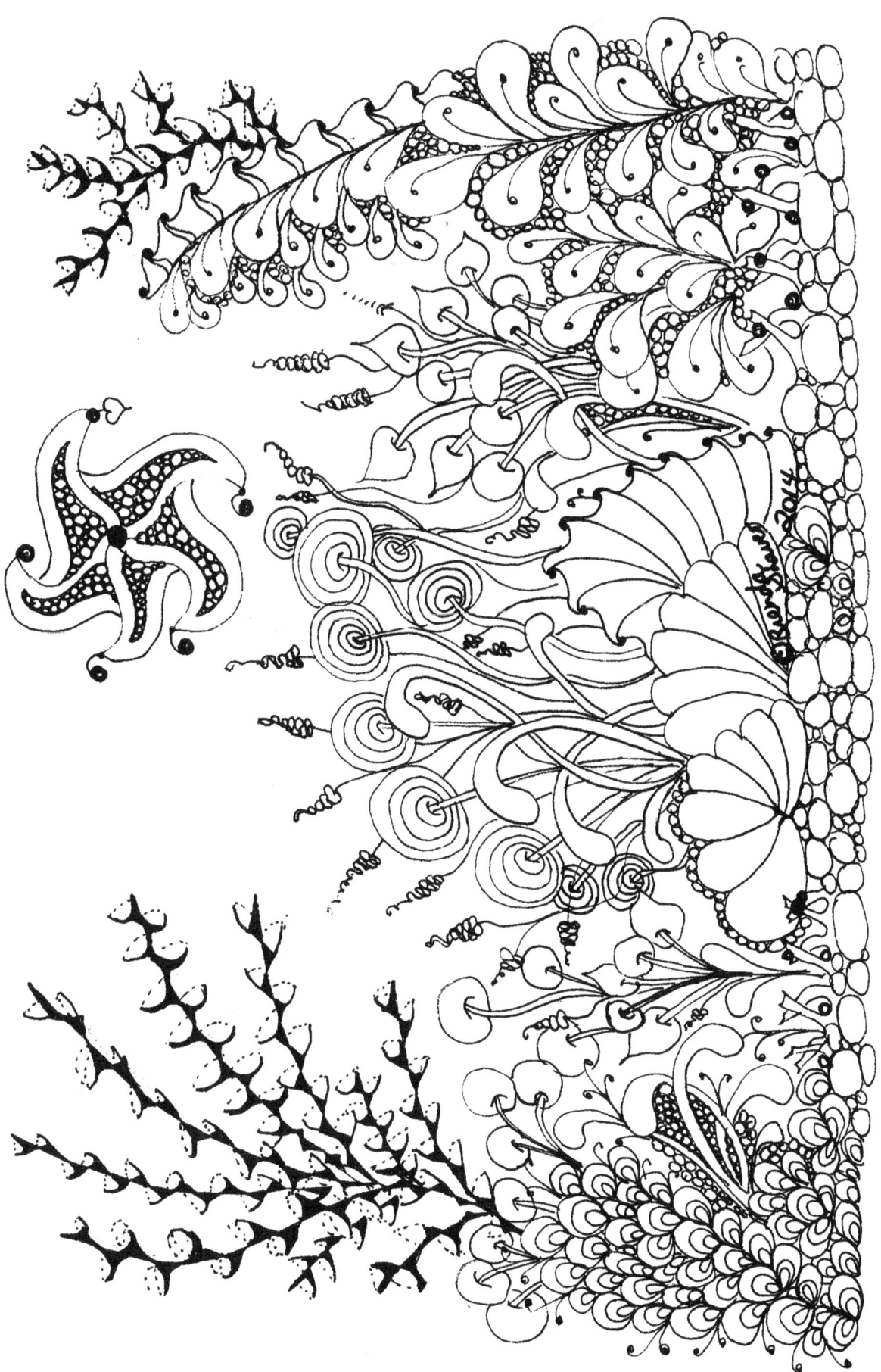

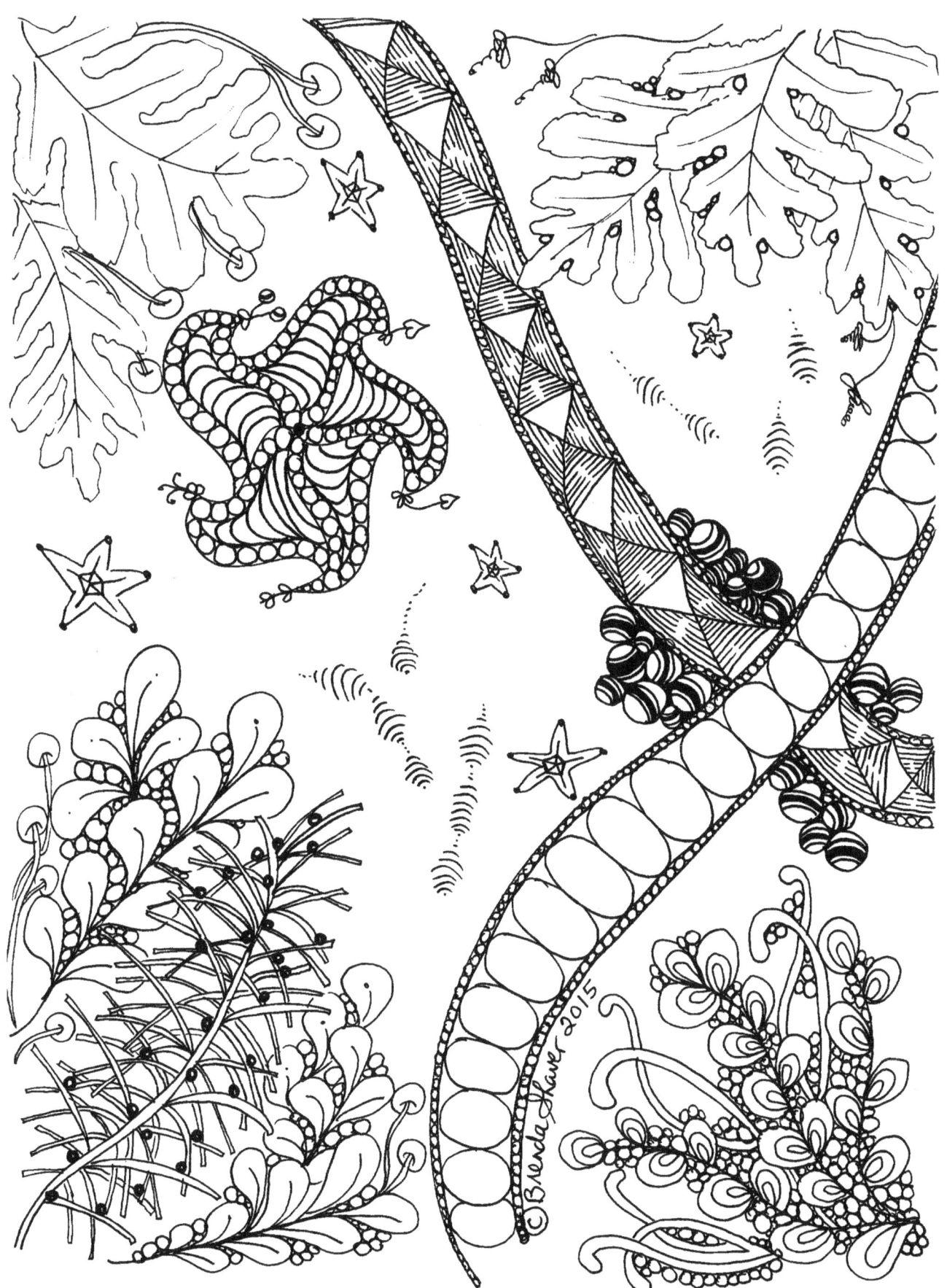

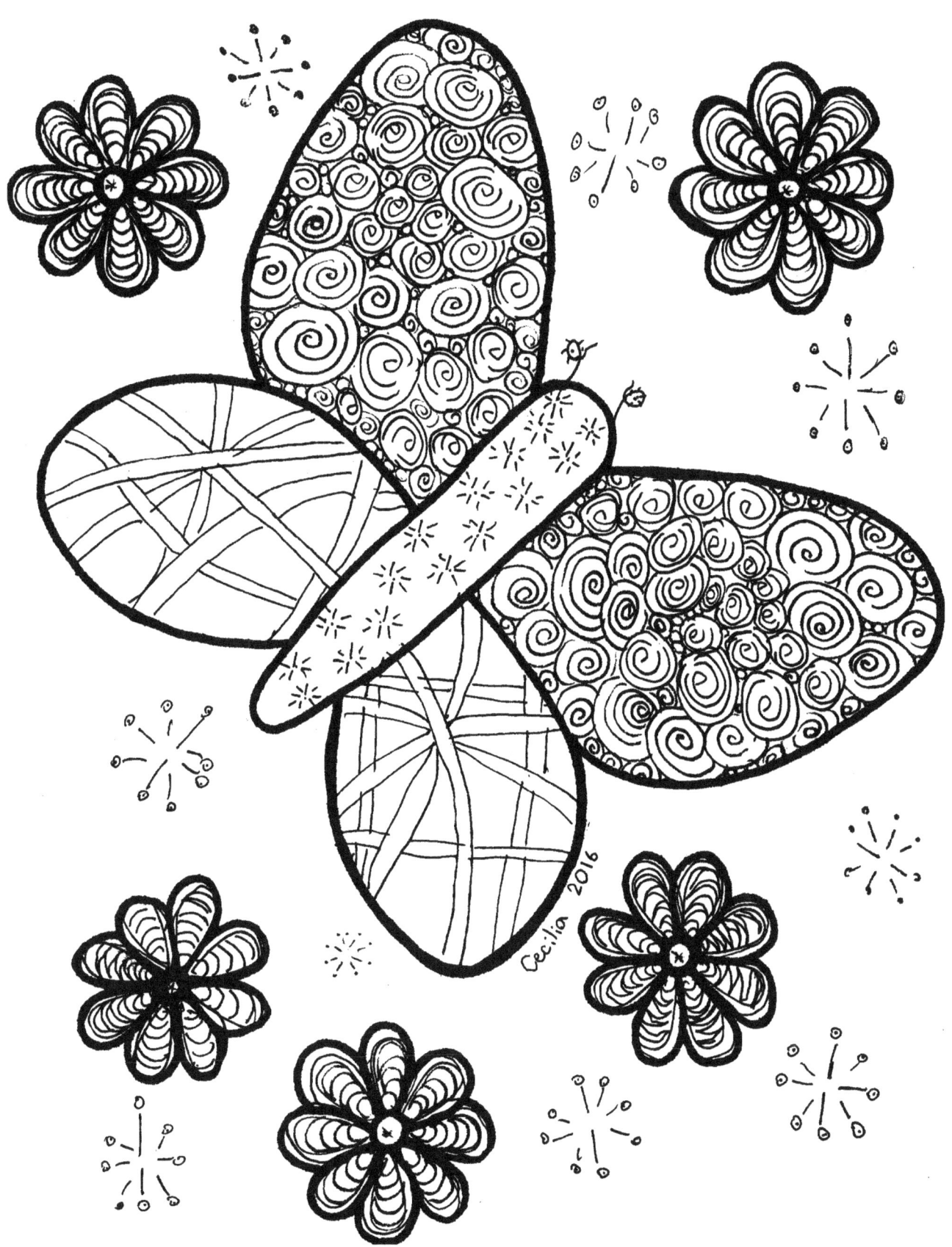

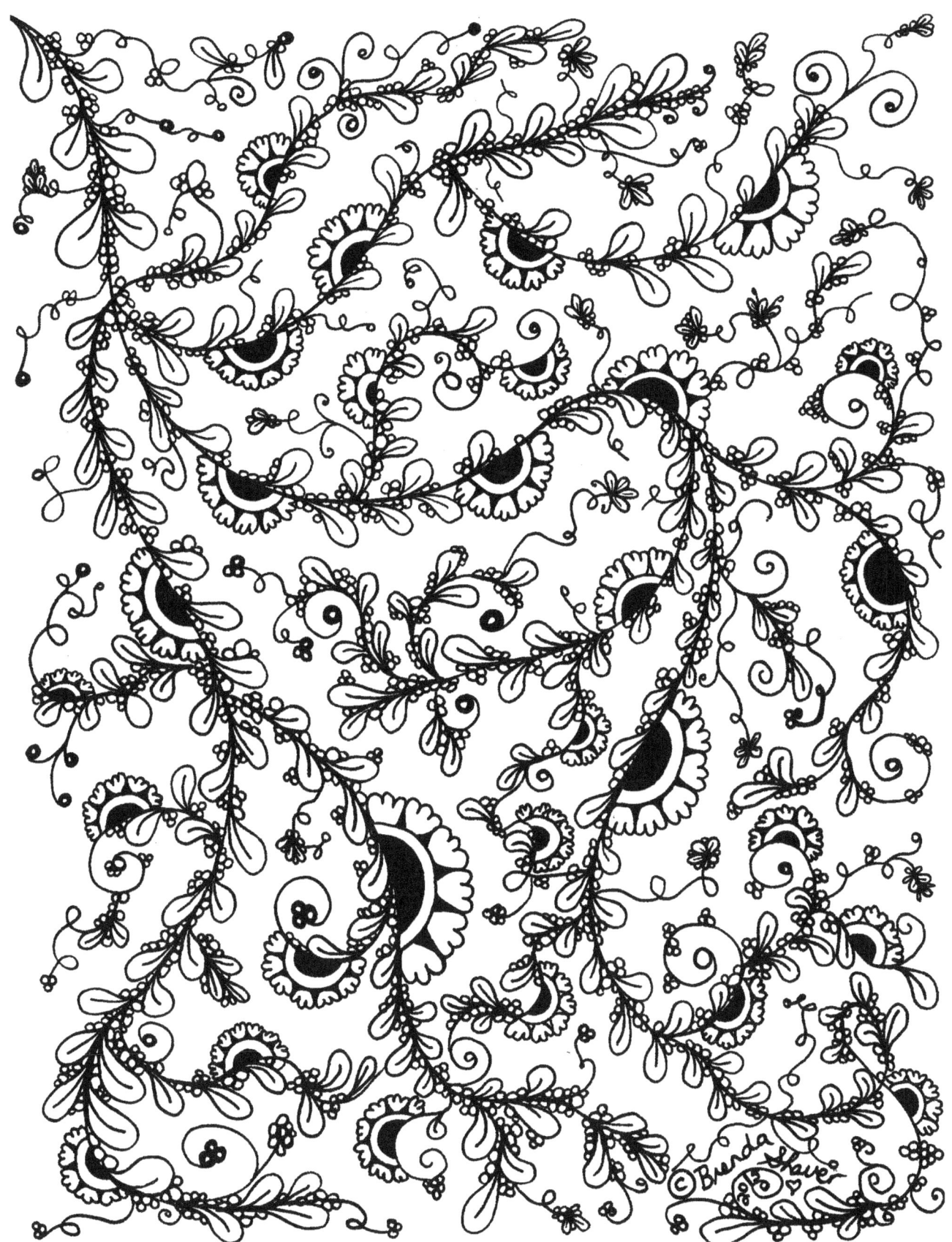

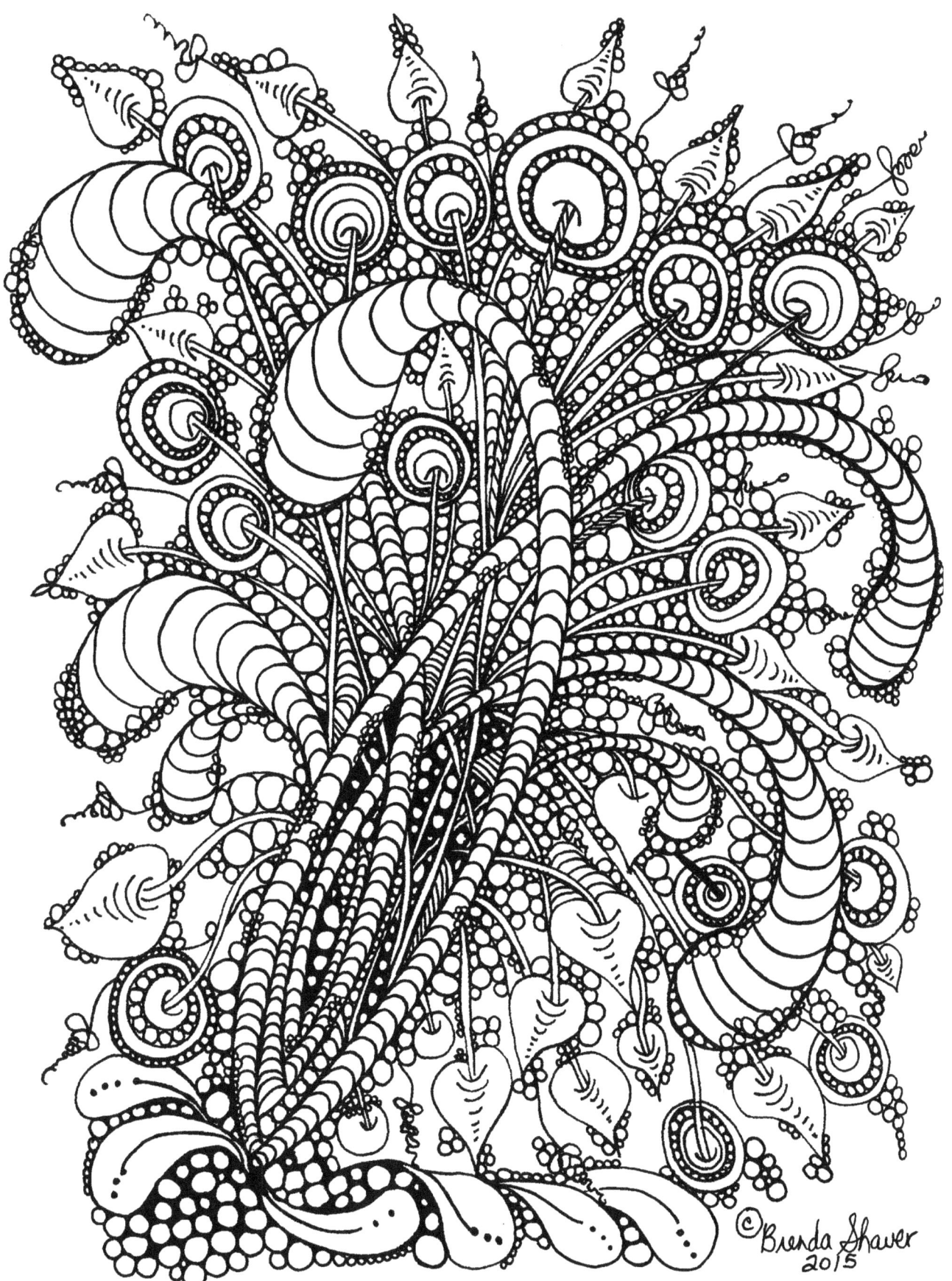

©Brenda Shaver
2015

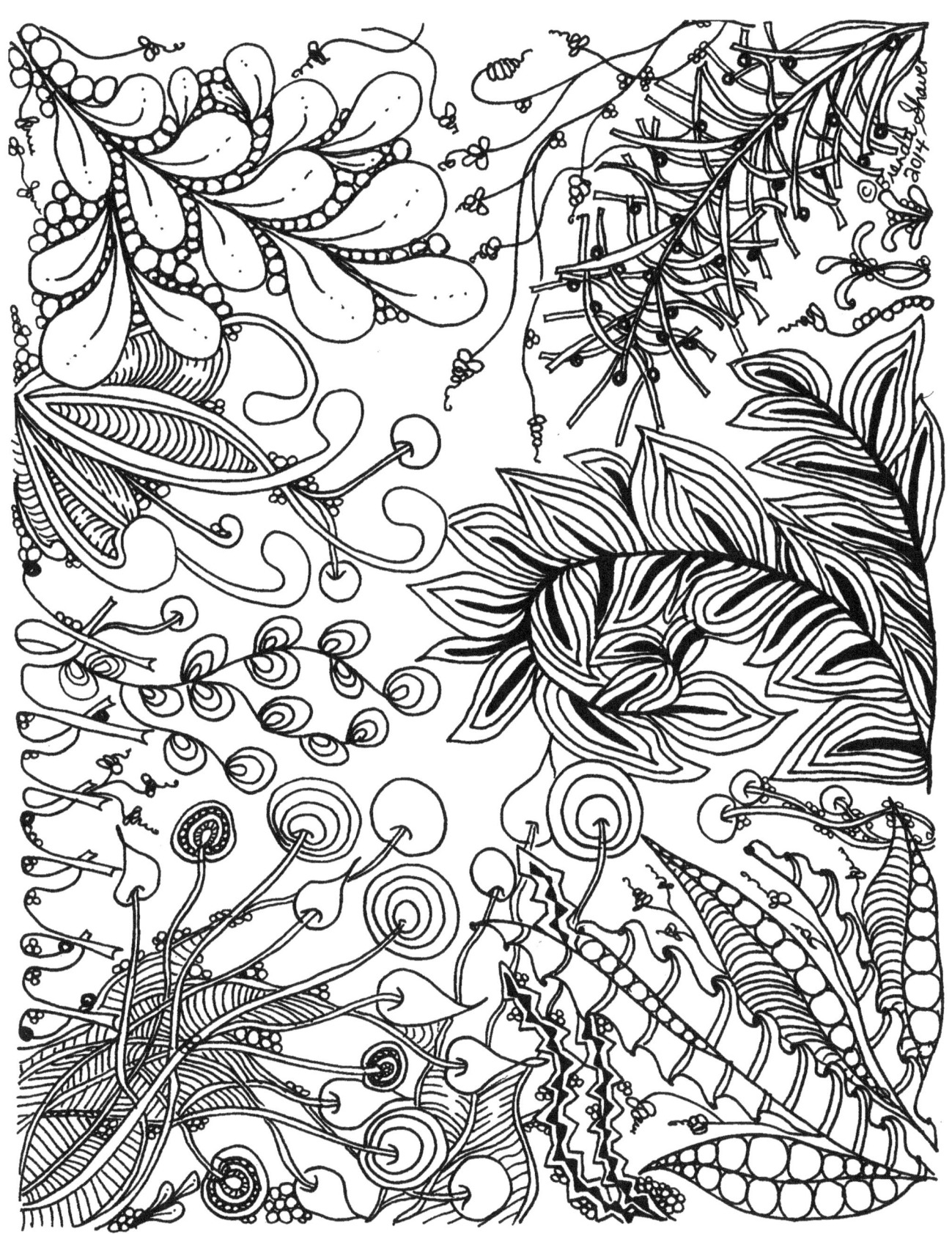

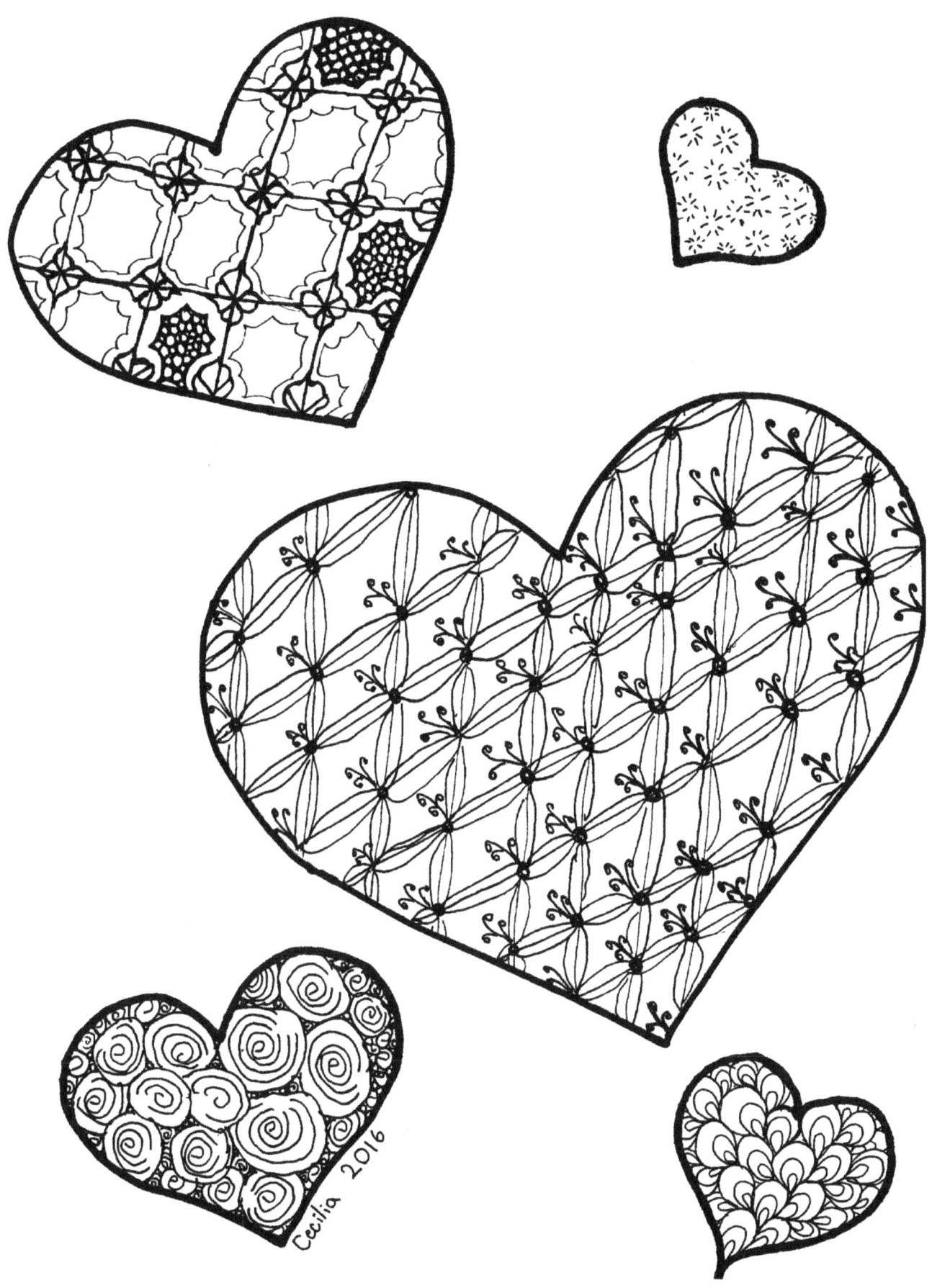

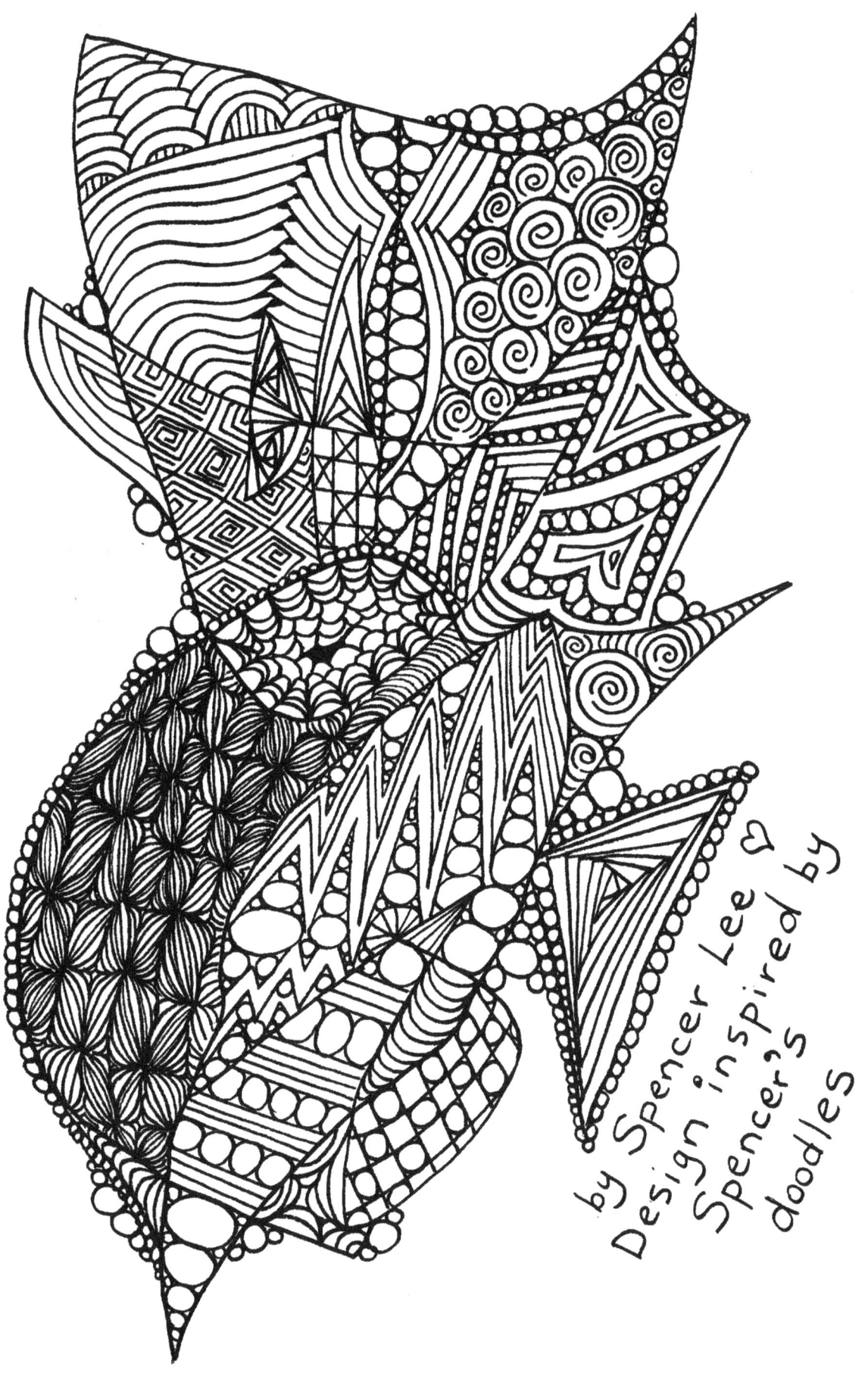

by Spencer Lee ♡
Design inspired by
Spencer's
doodles

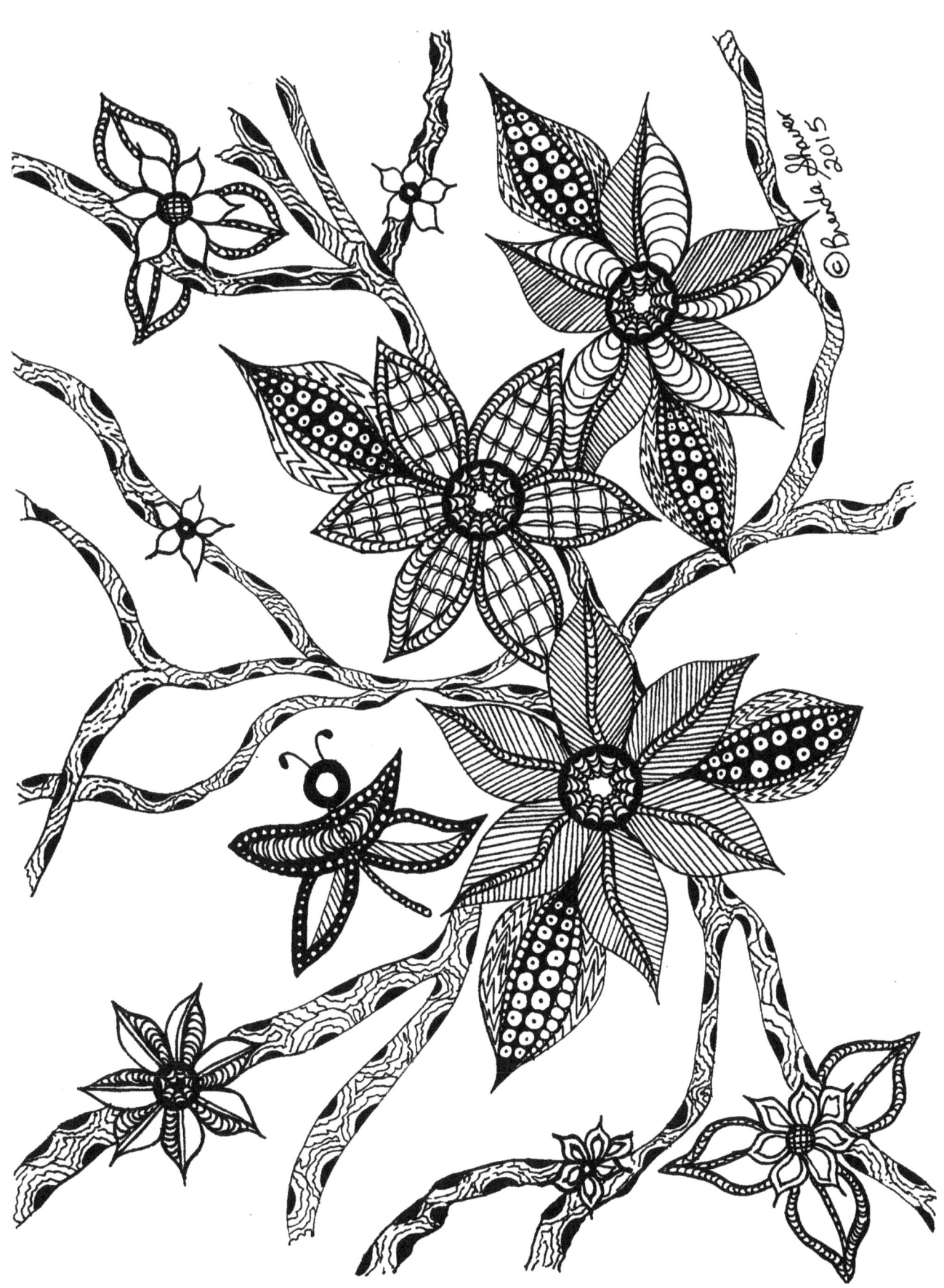

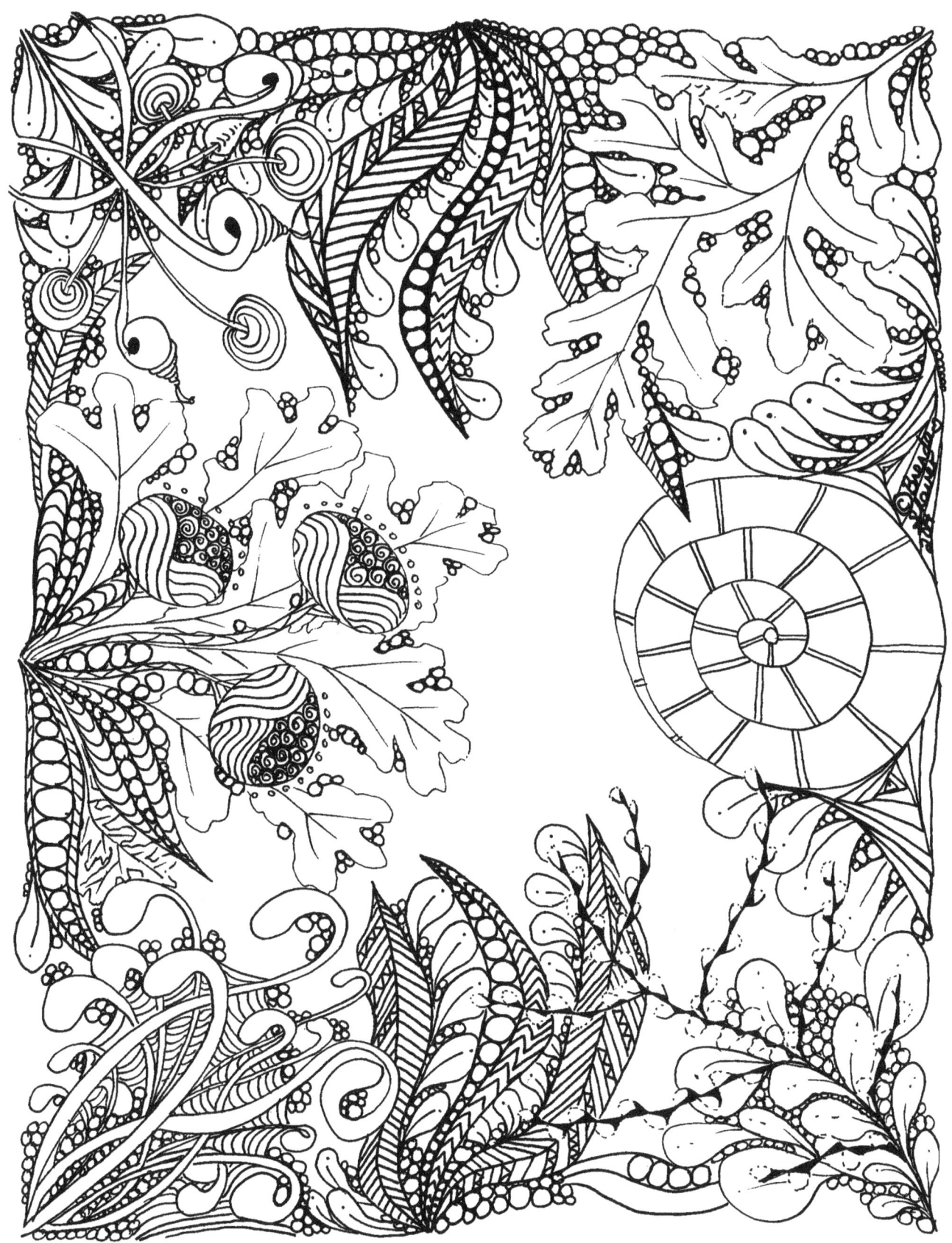

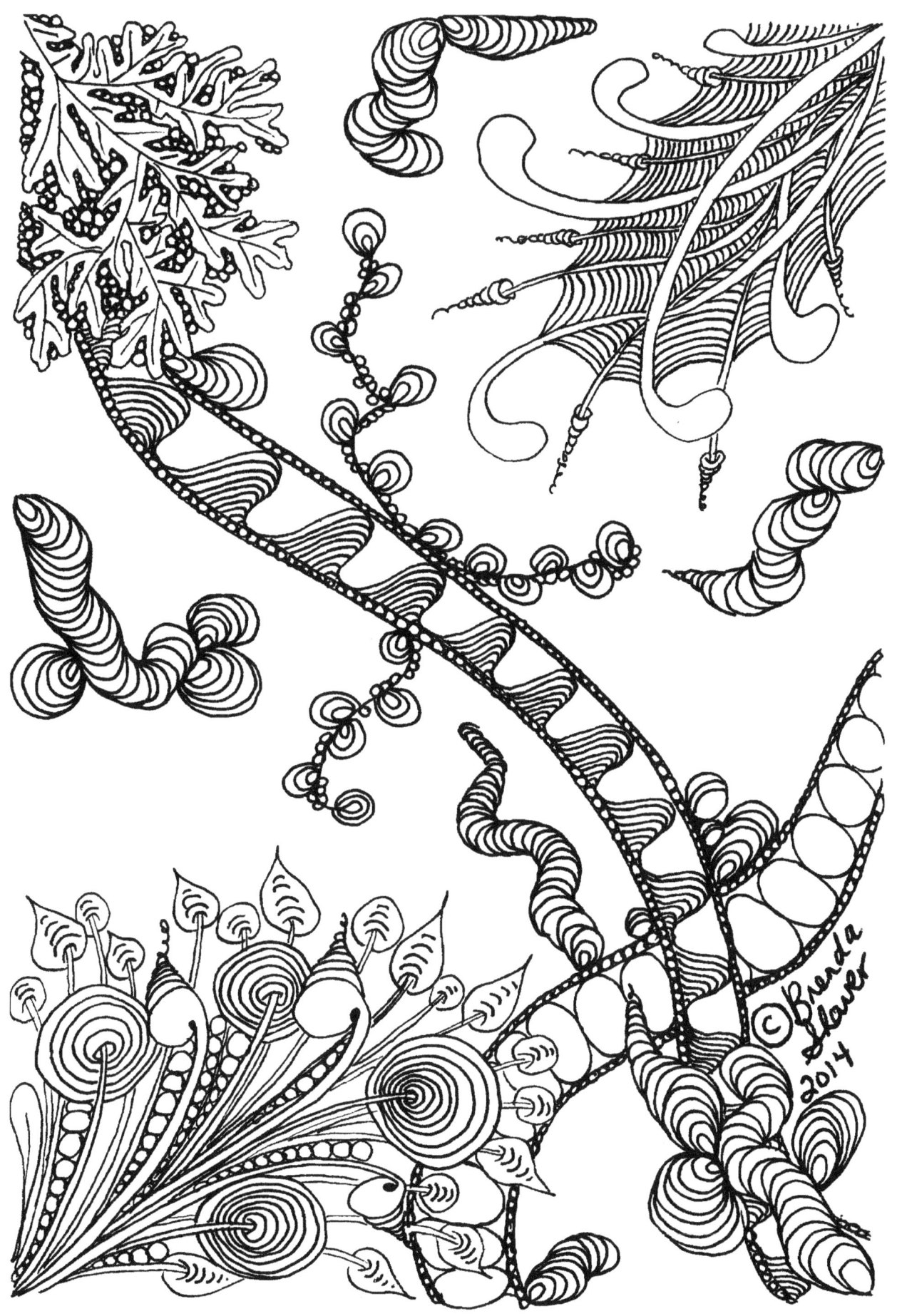

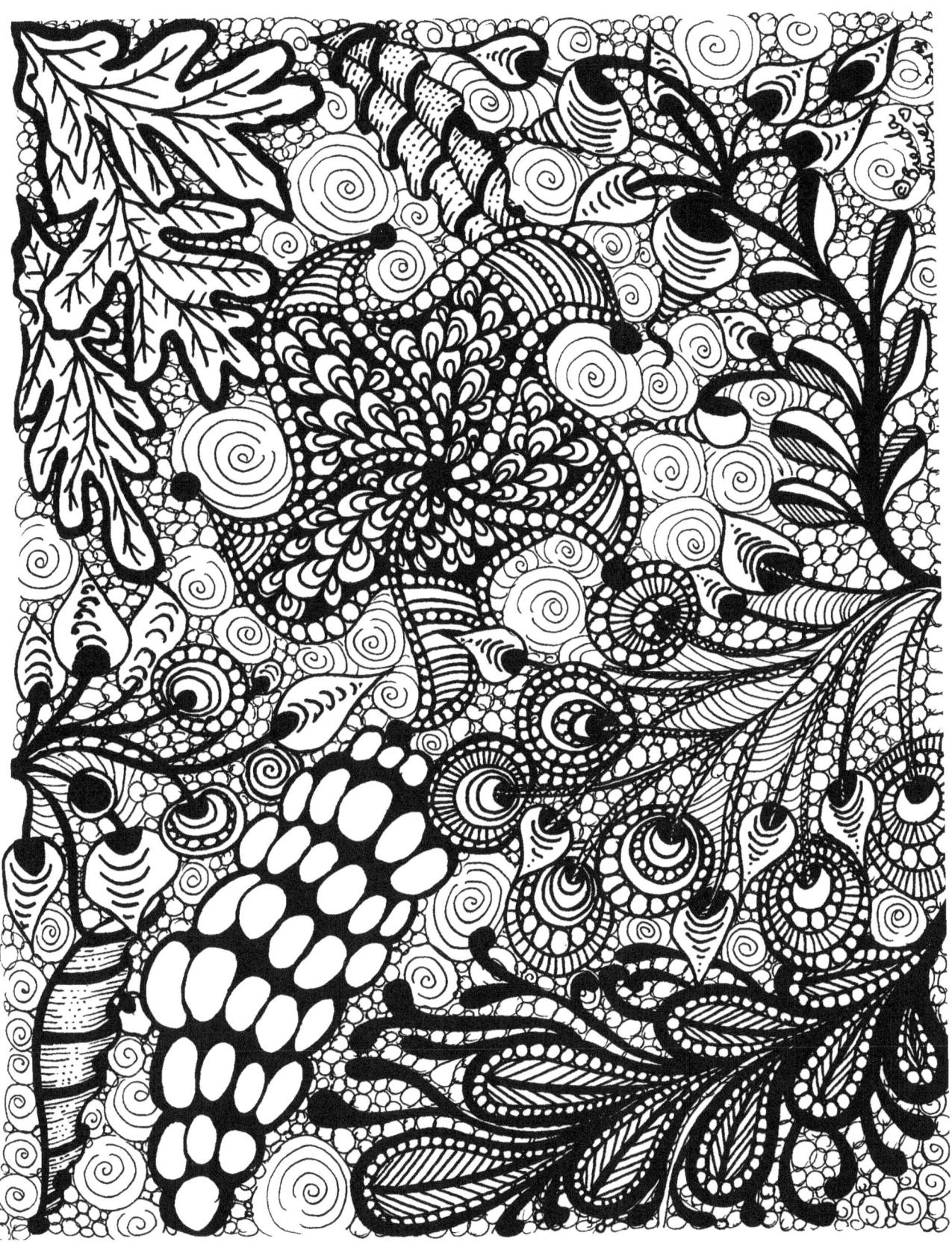

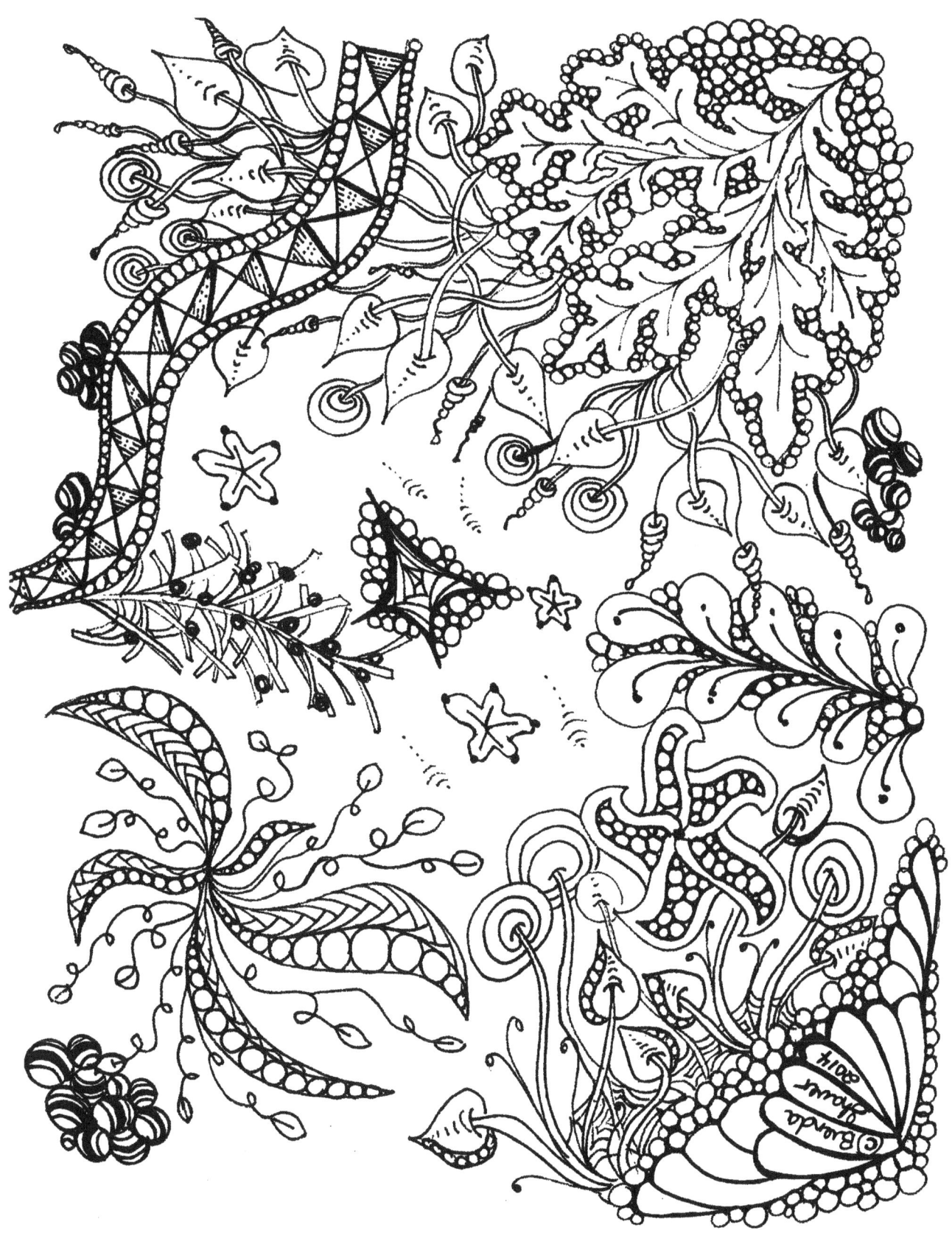

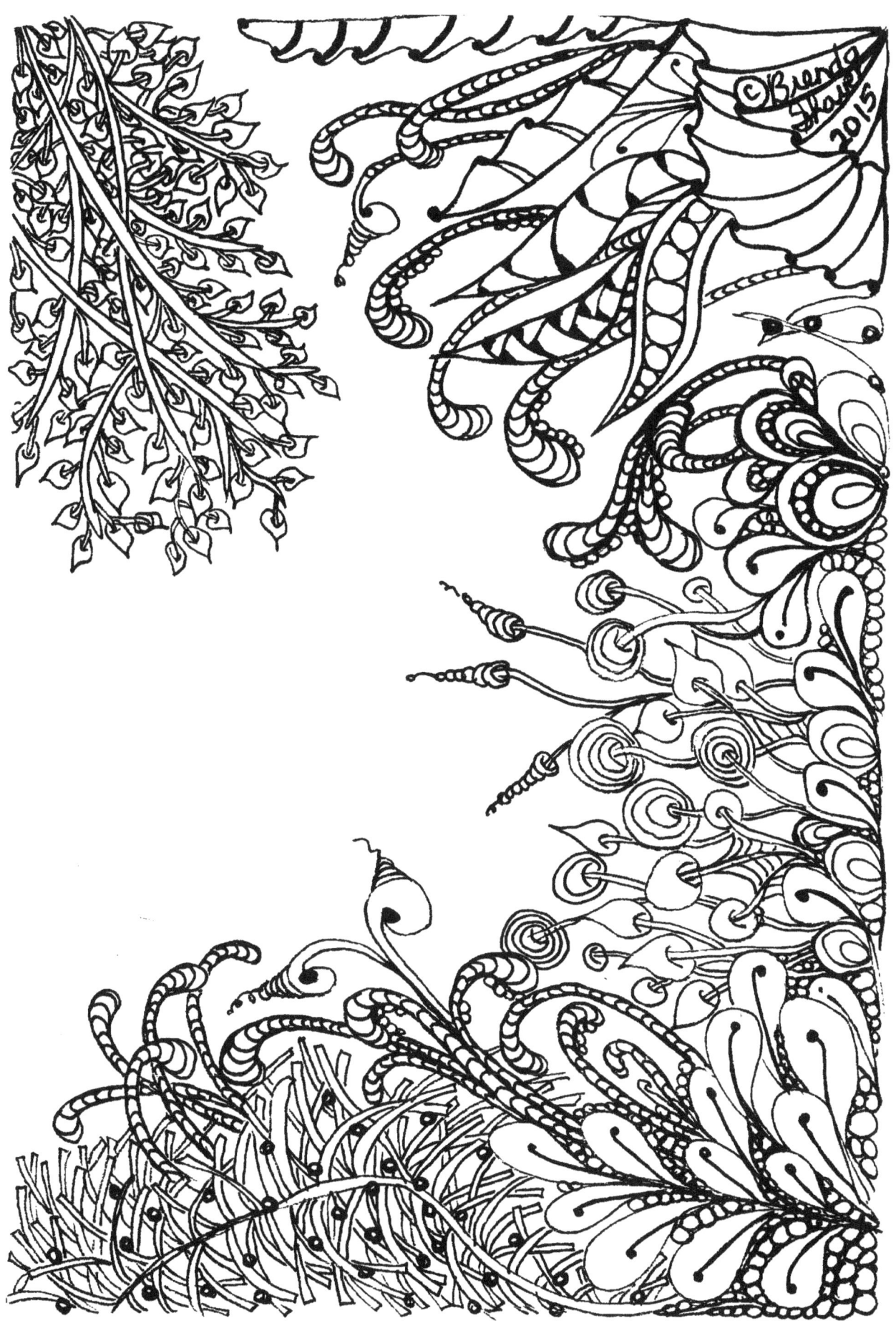

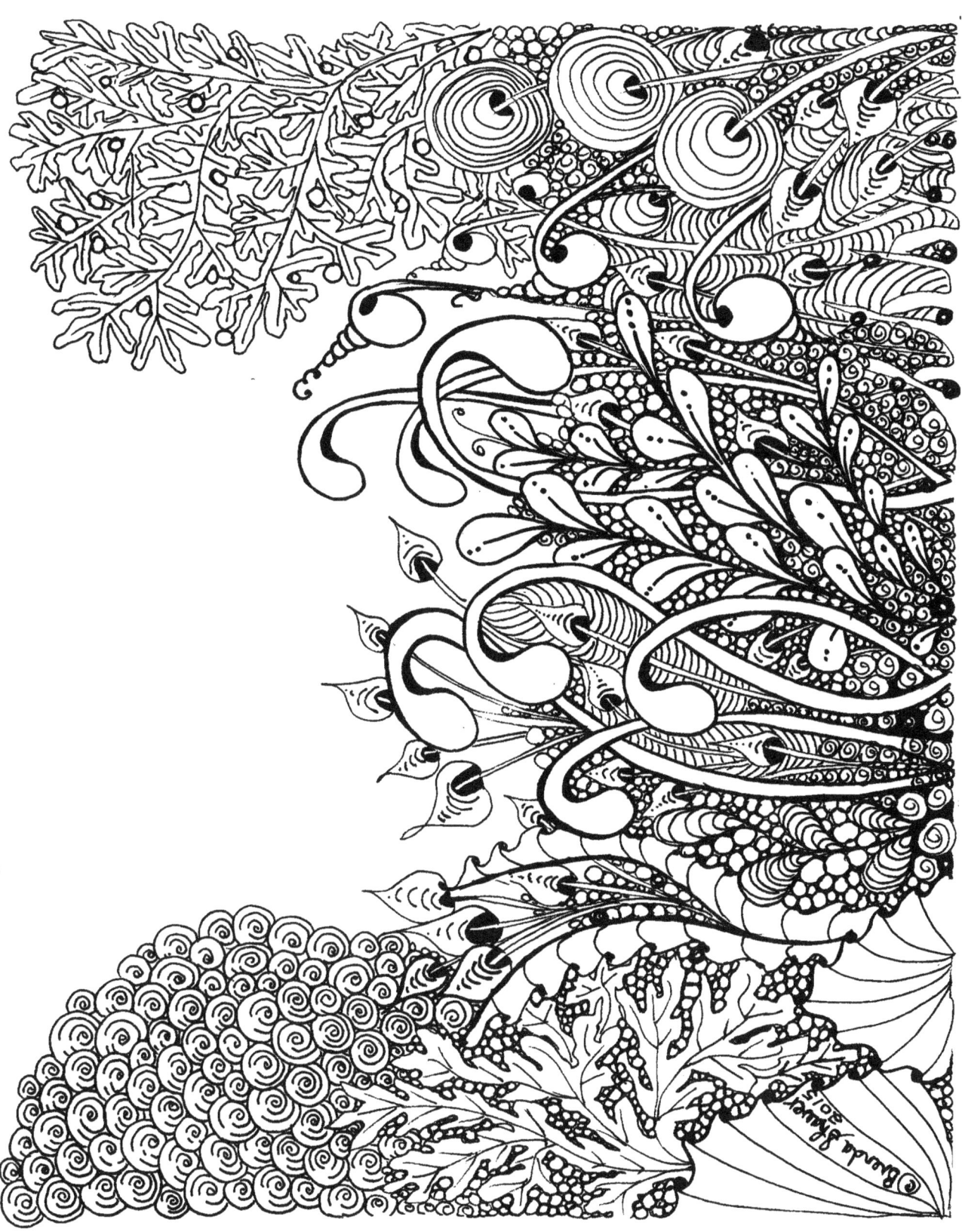

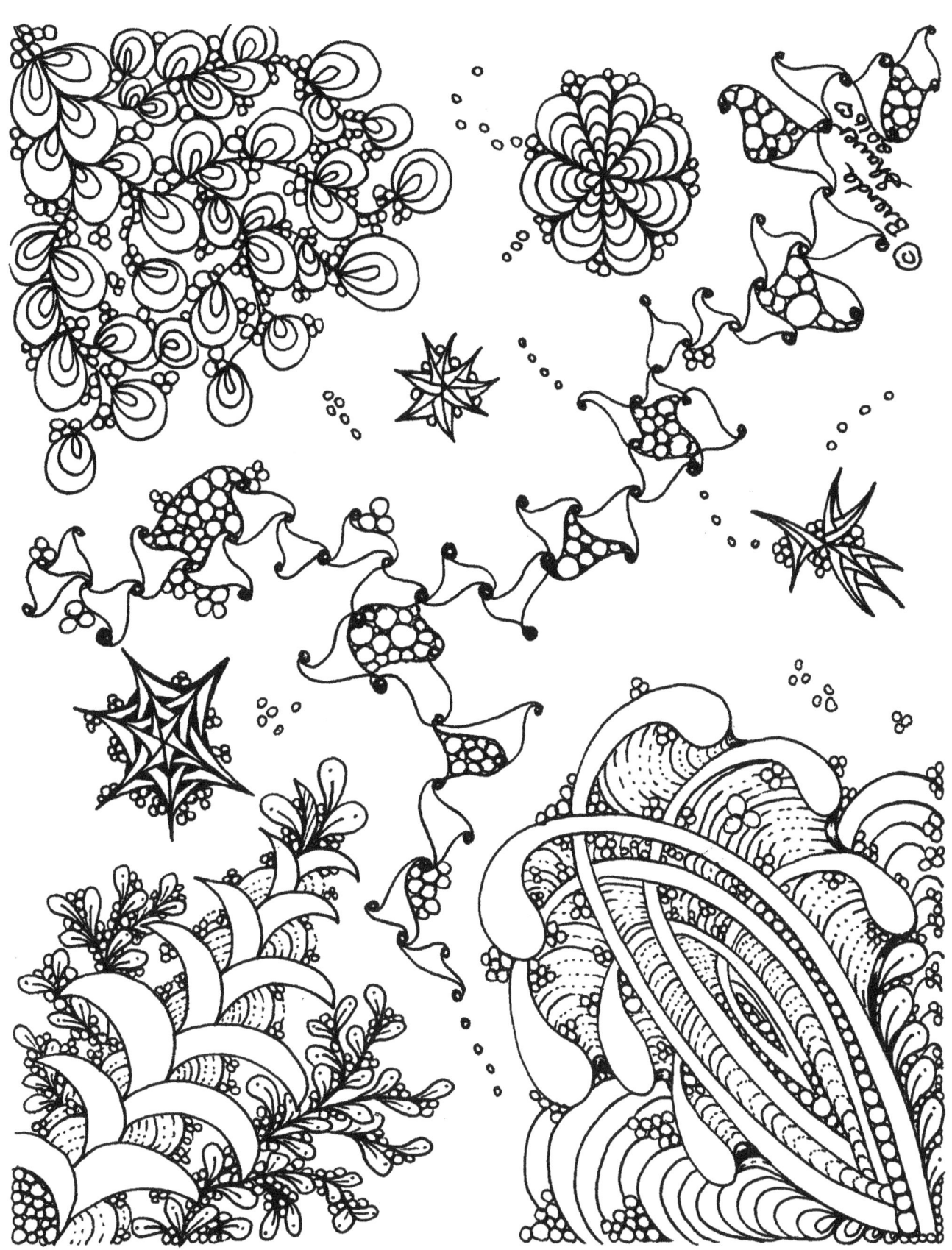

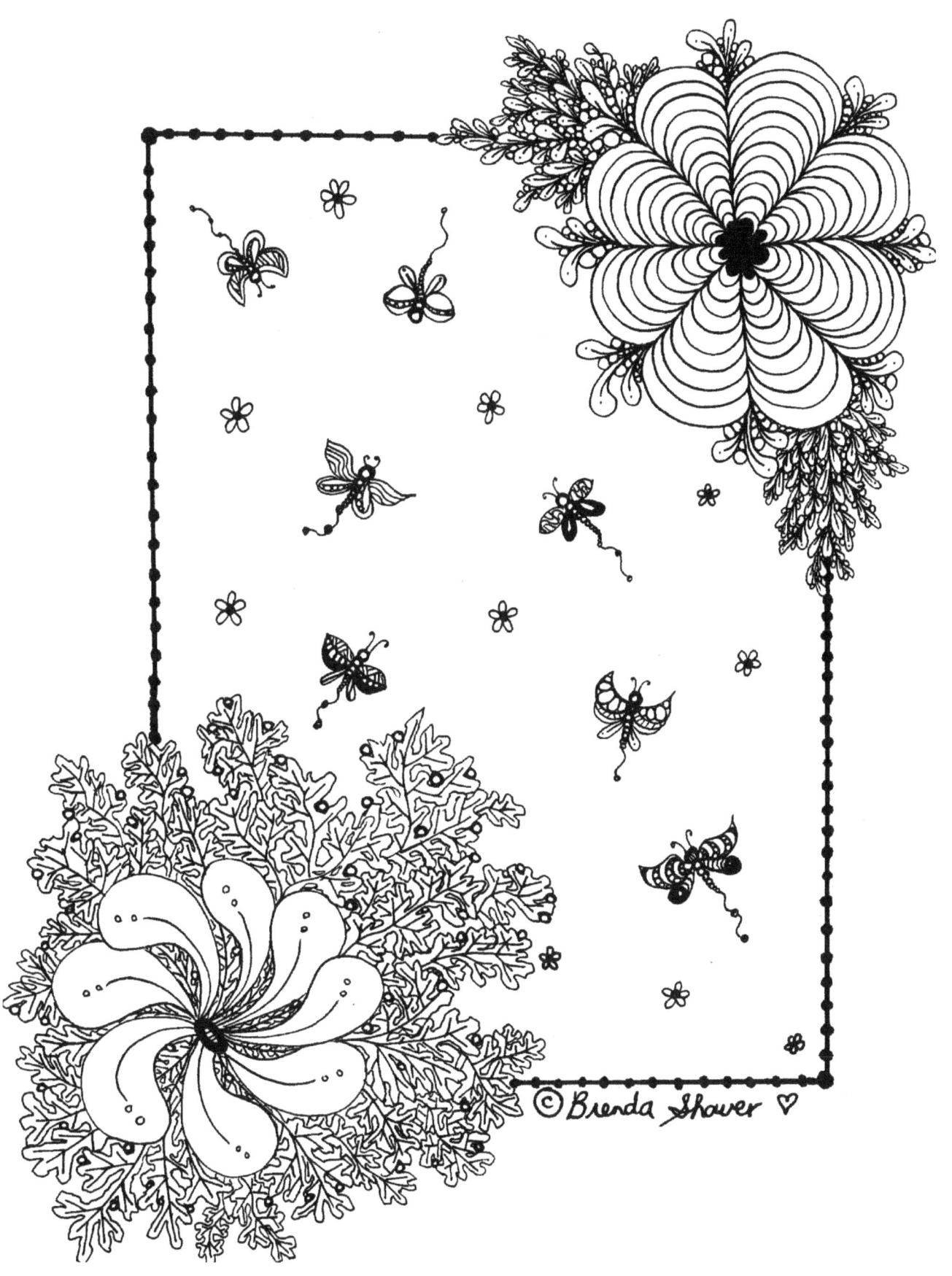

© Brenda Shaver ♡

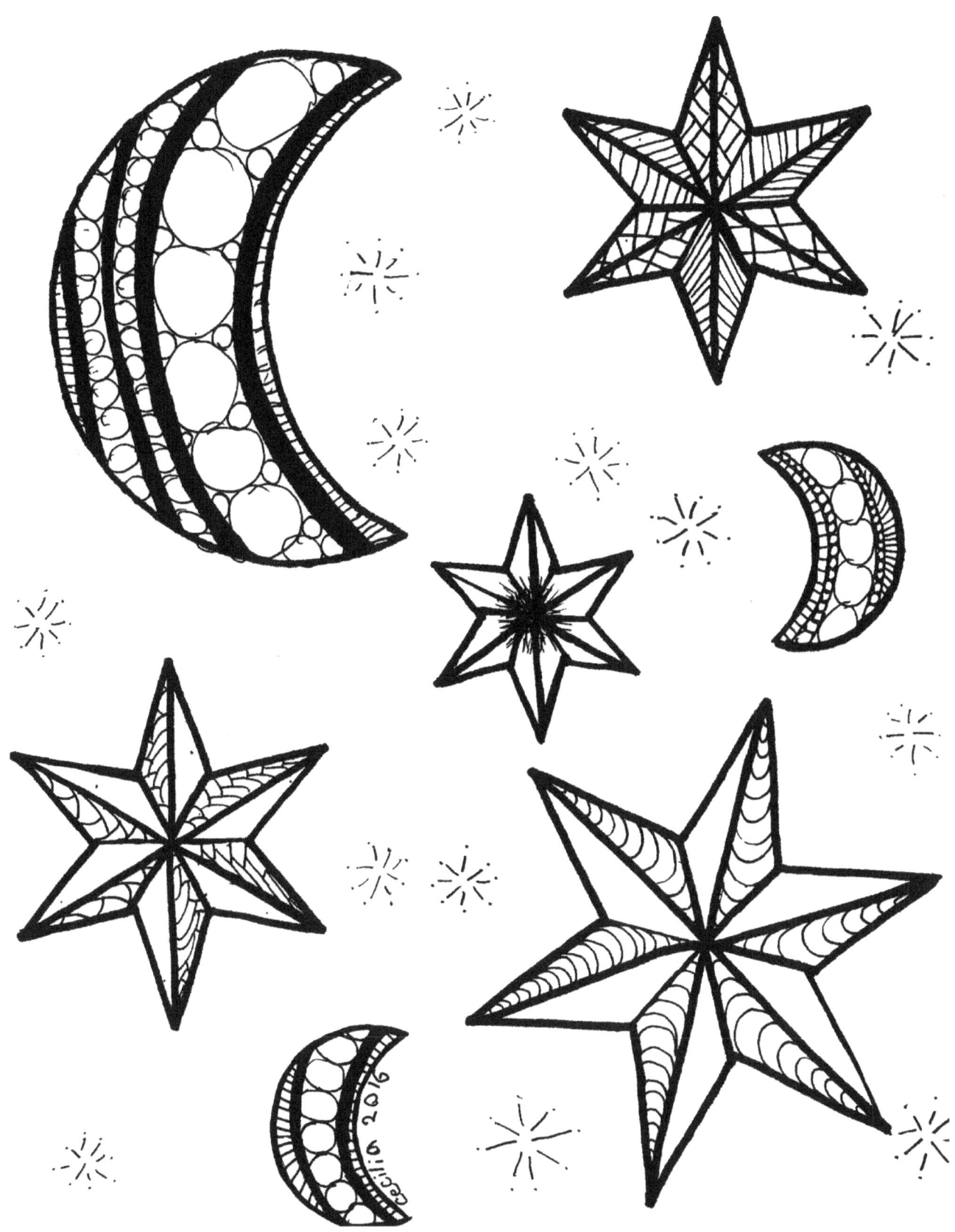

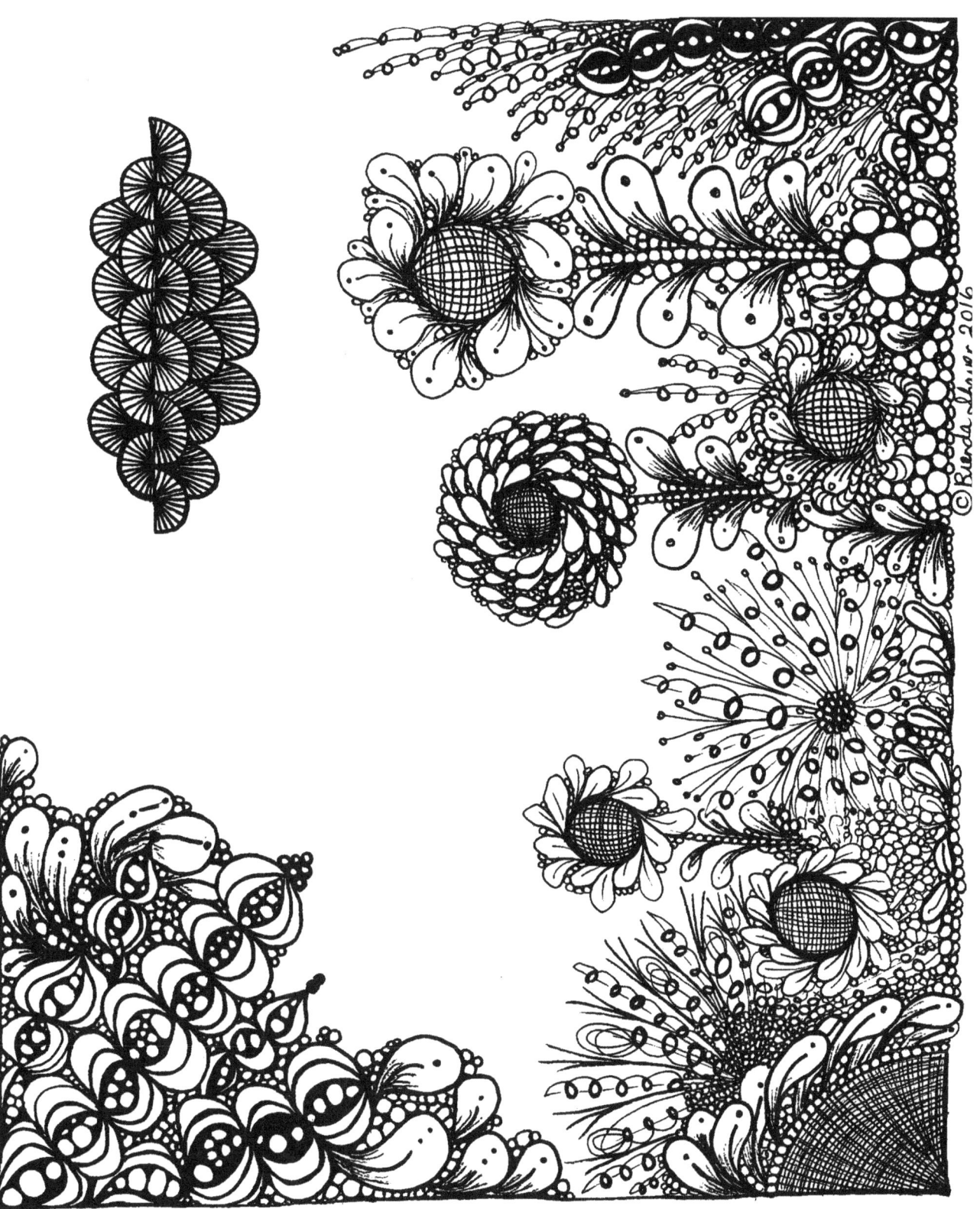

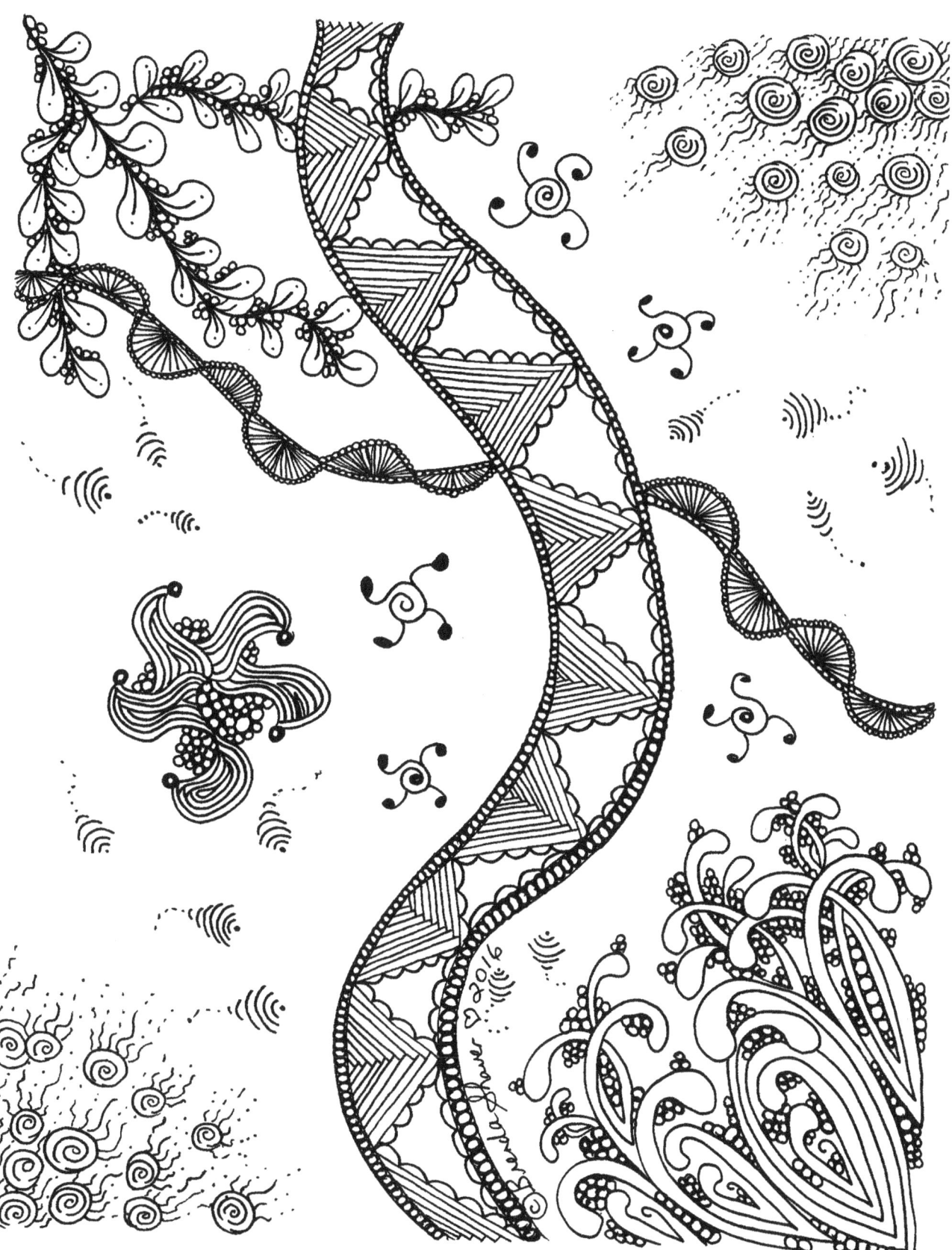

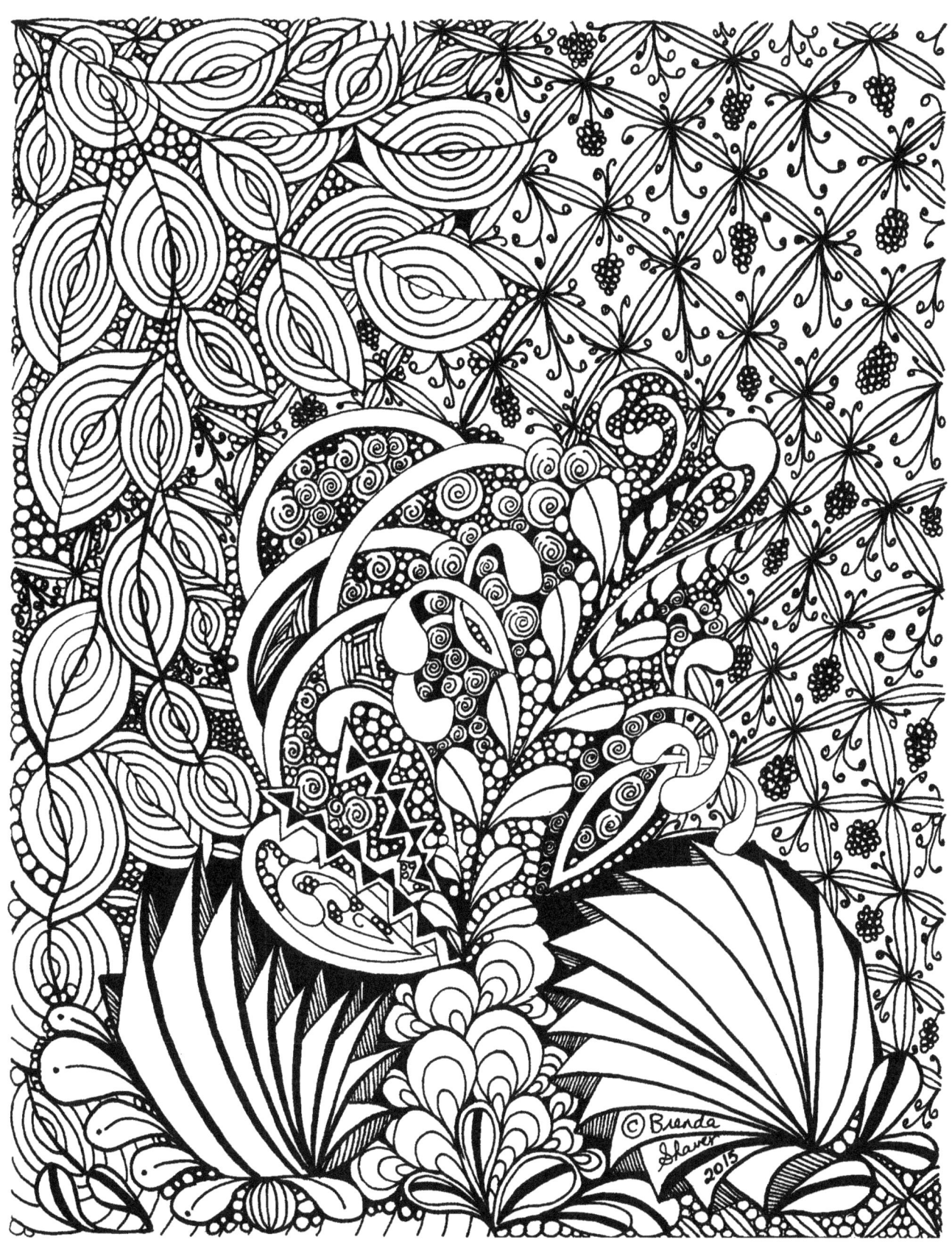

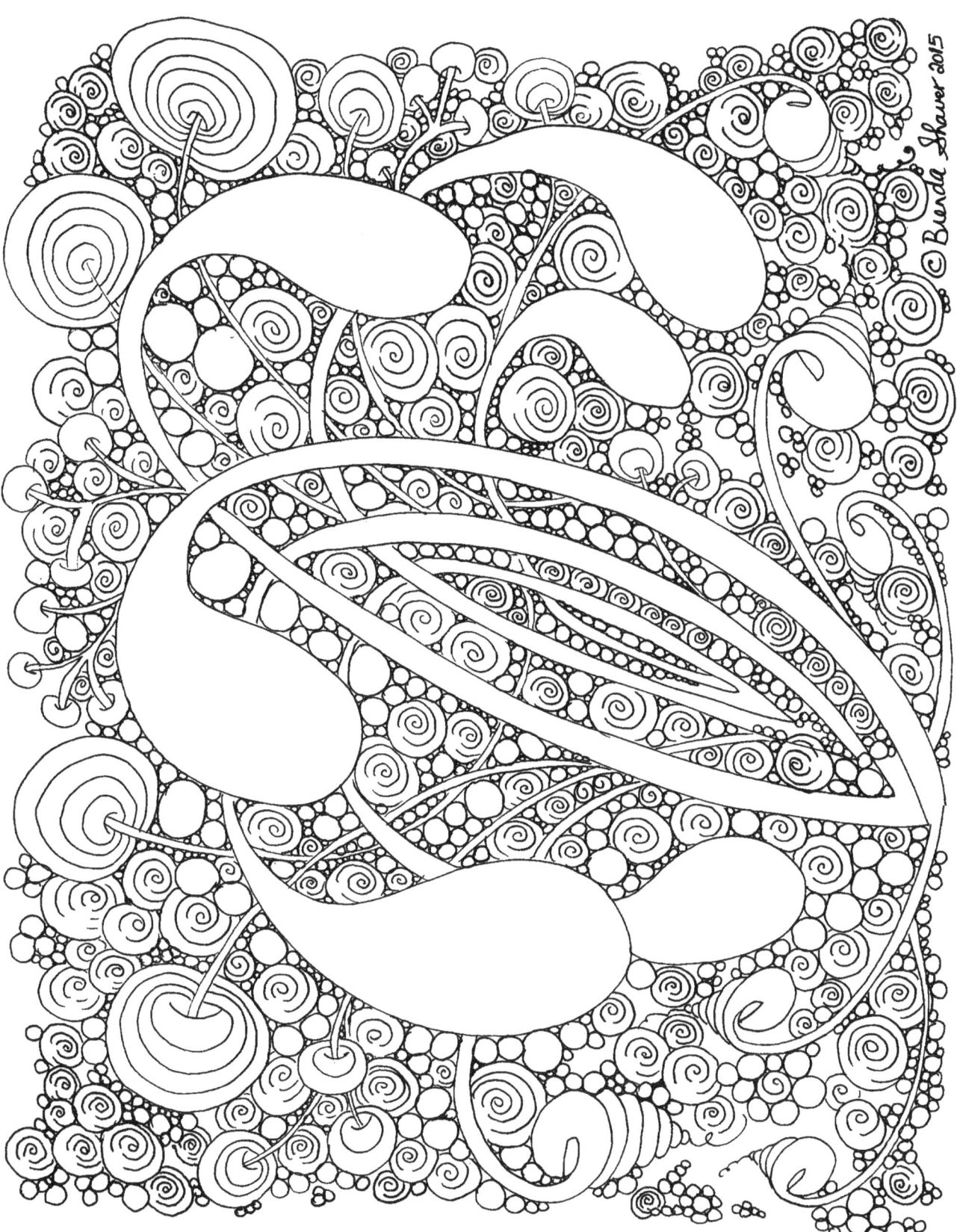
© Brenda Shaver 2015

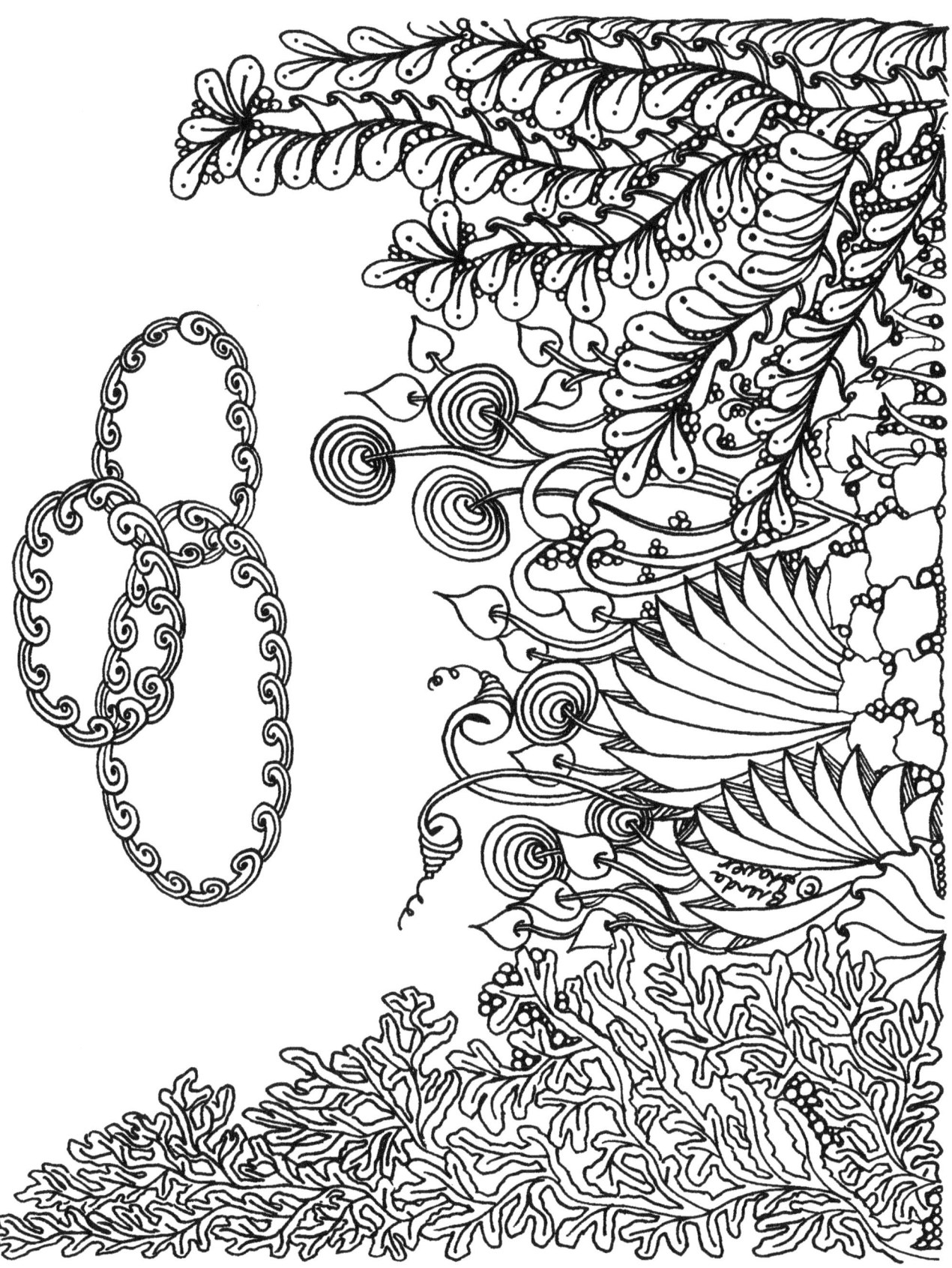

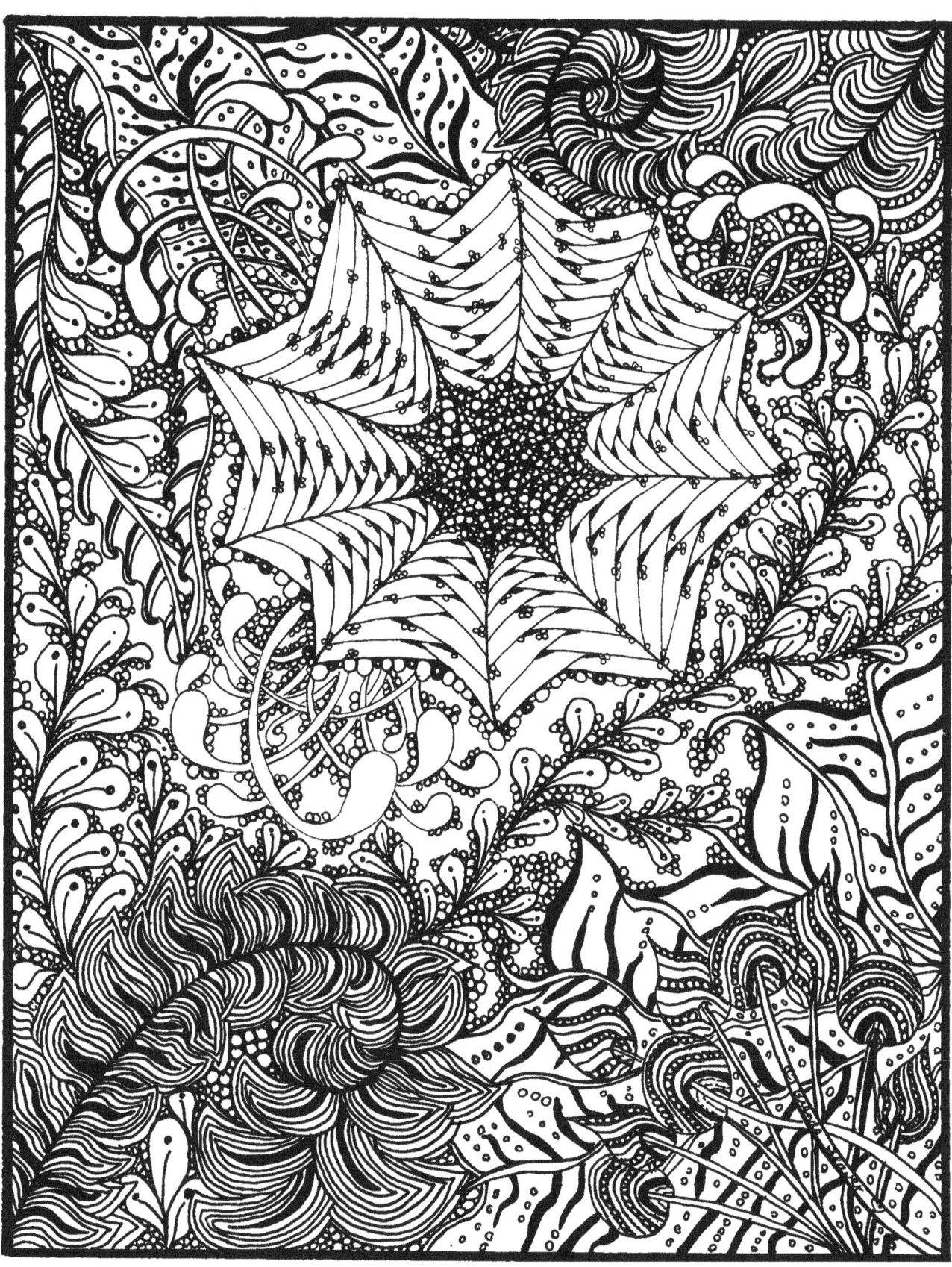

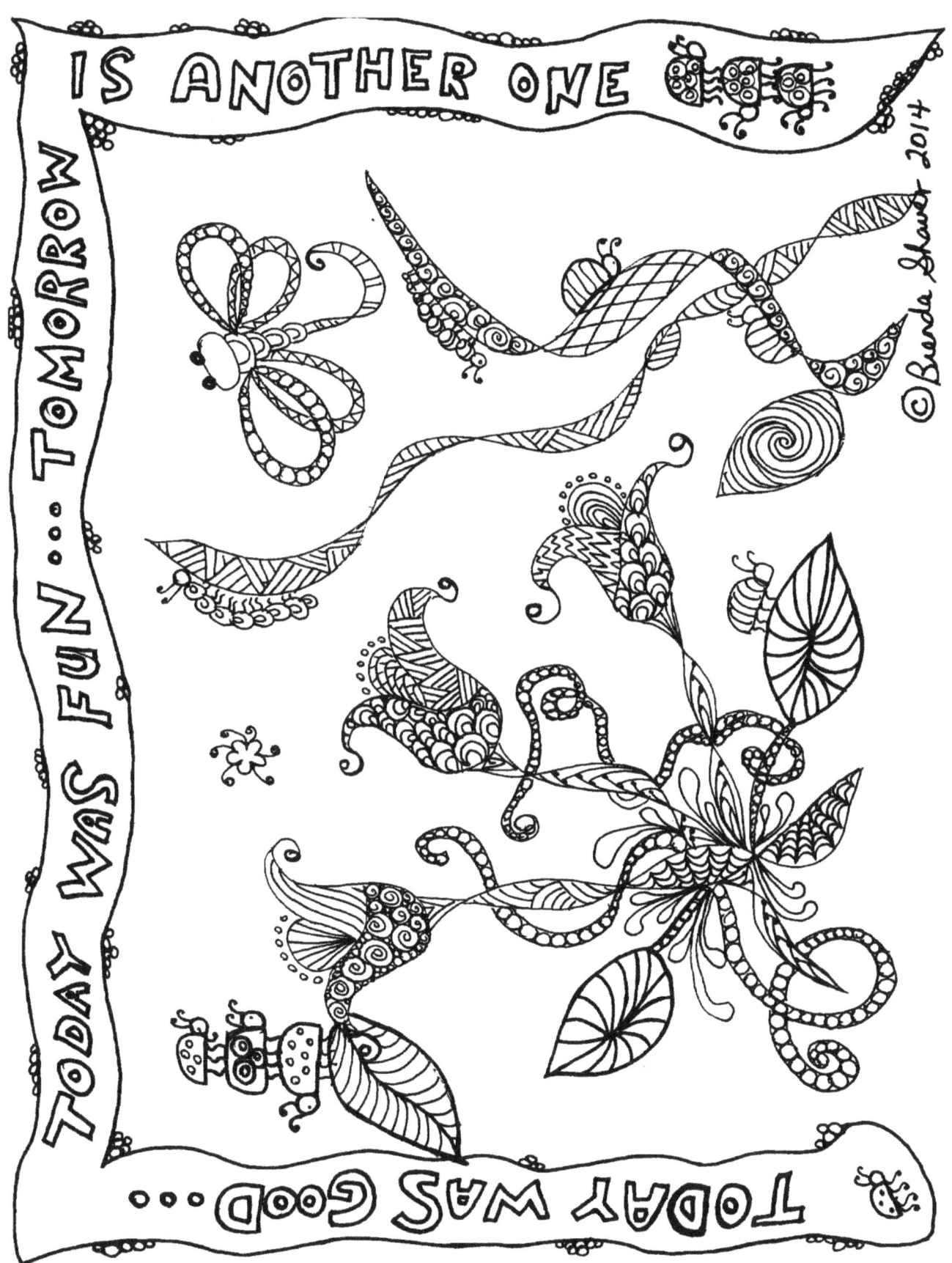

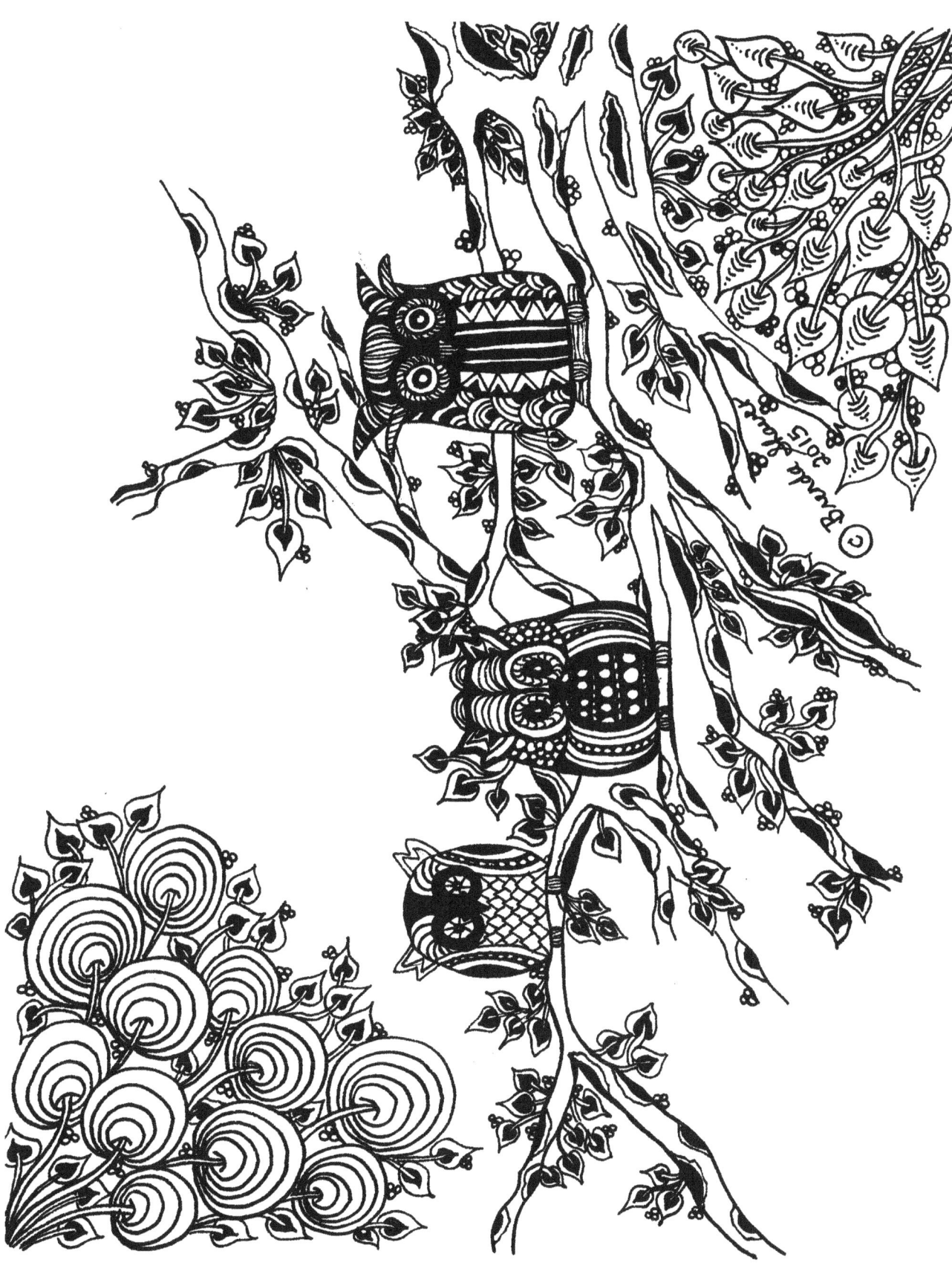

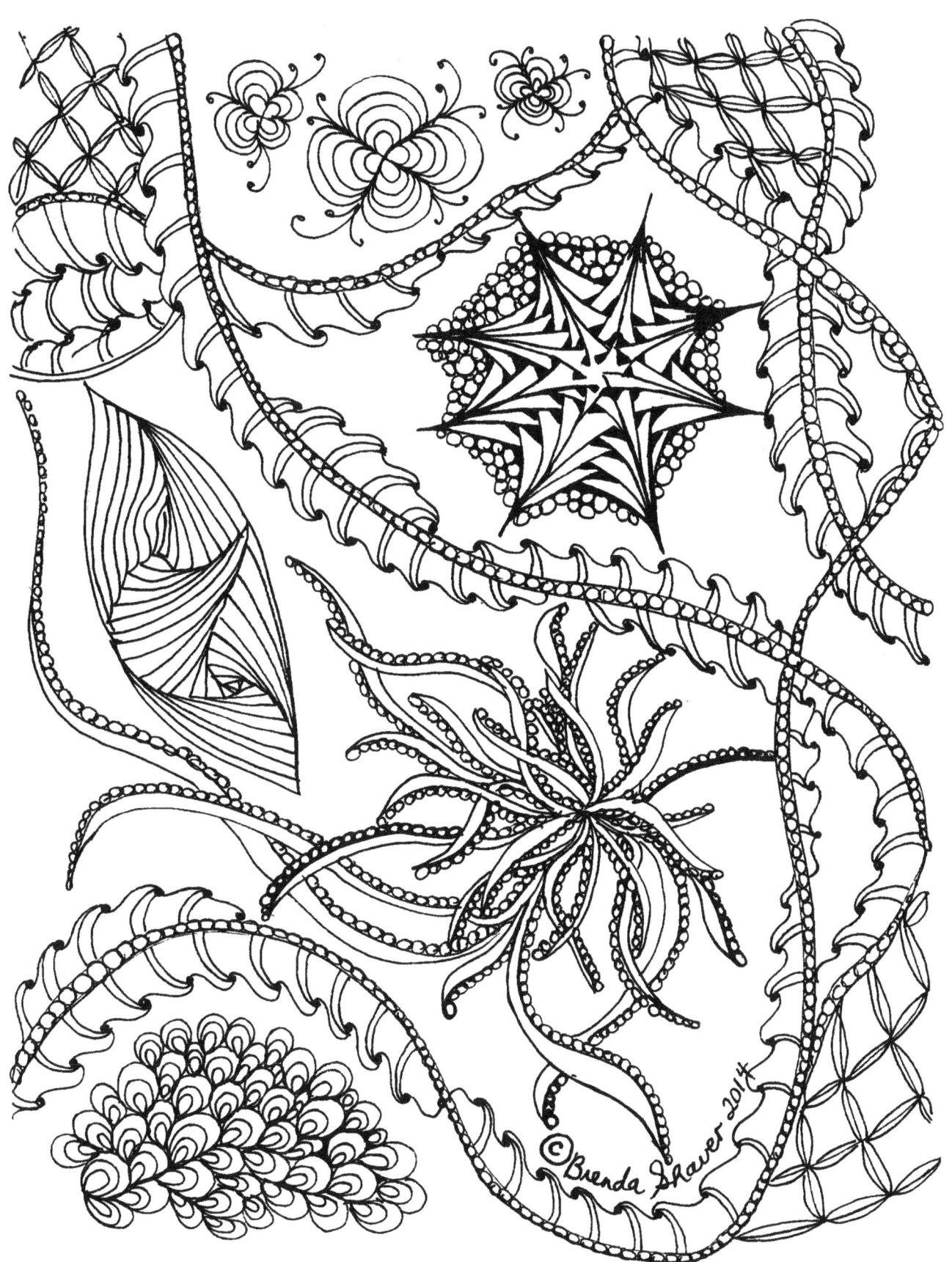

©Brenda Shaver 2014

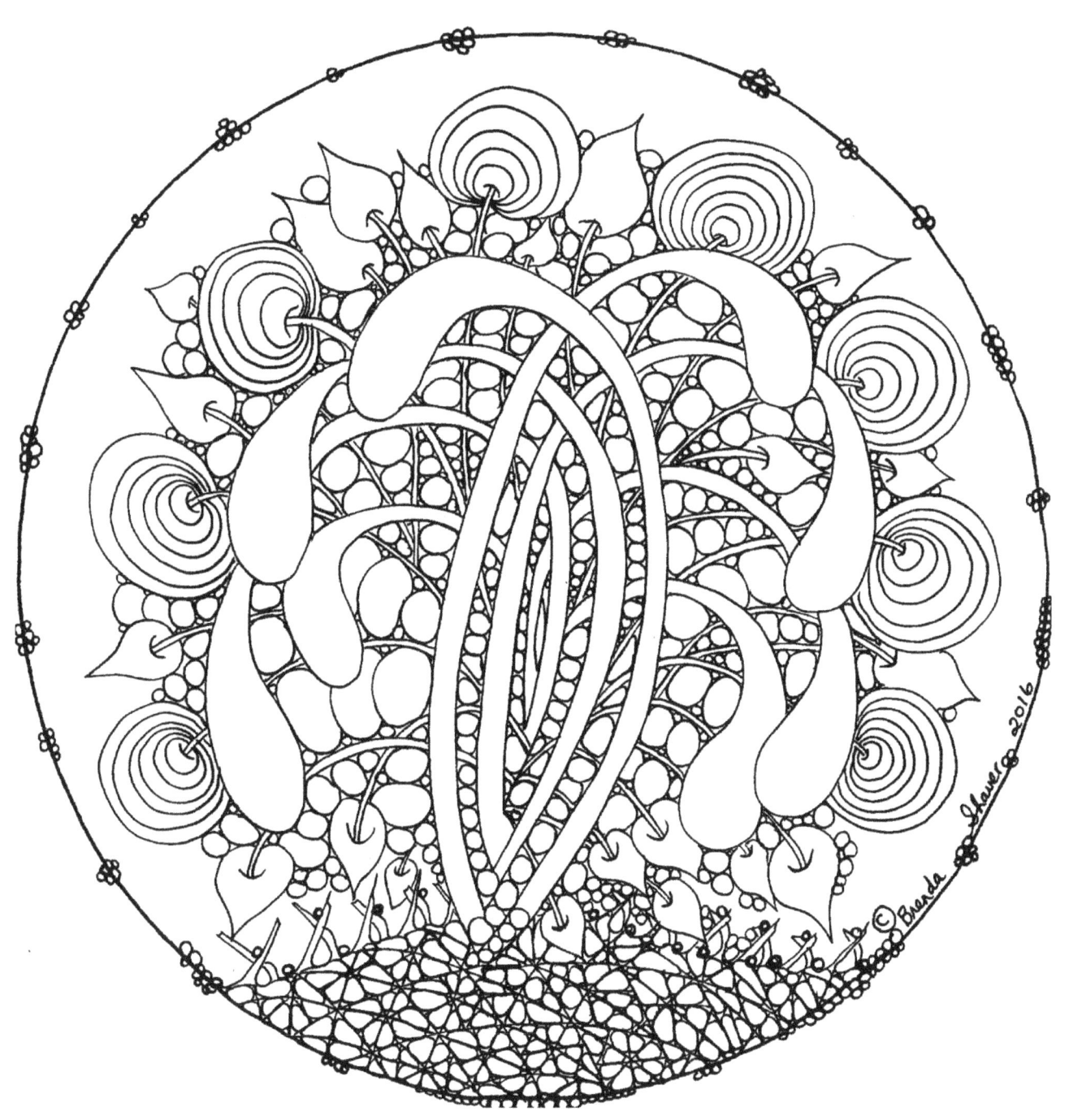

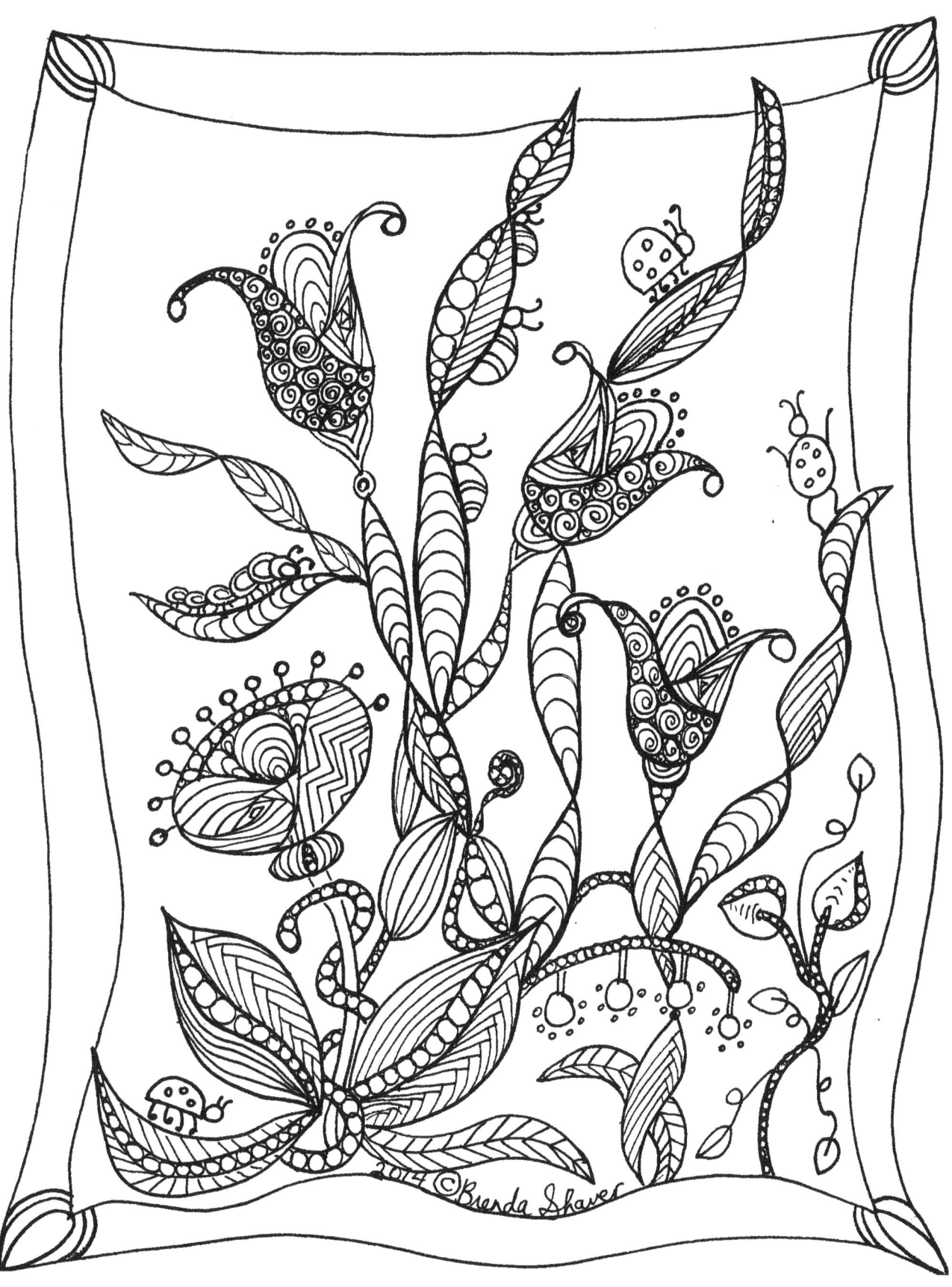

©Brenda Shaver

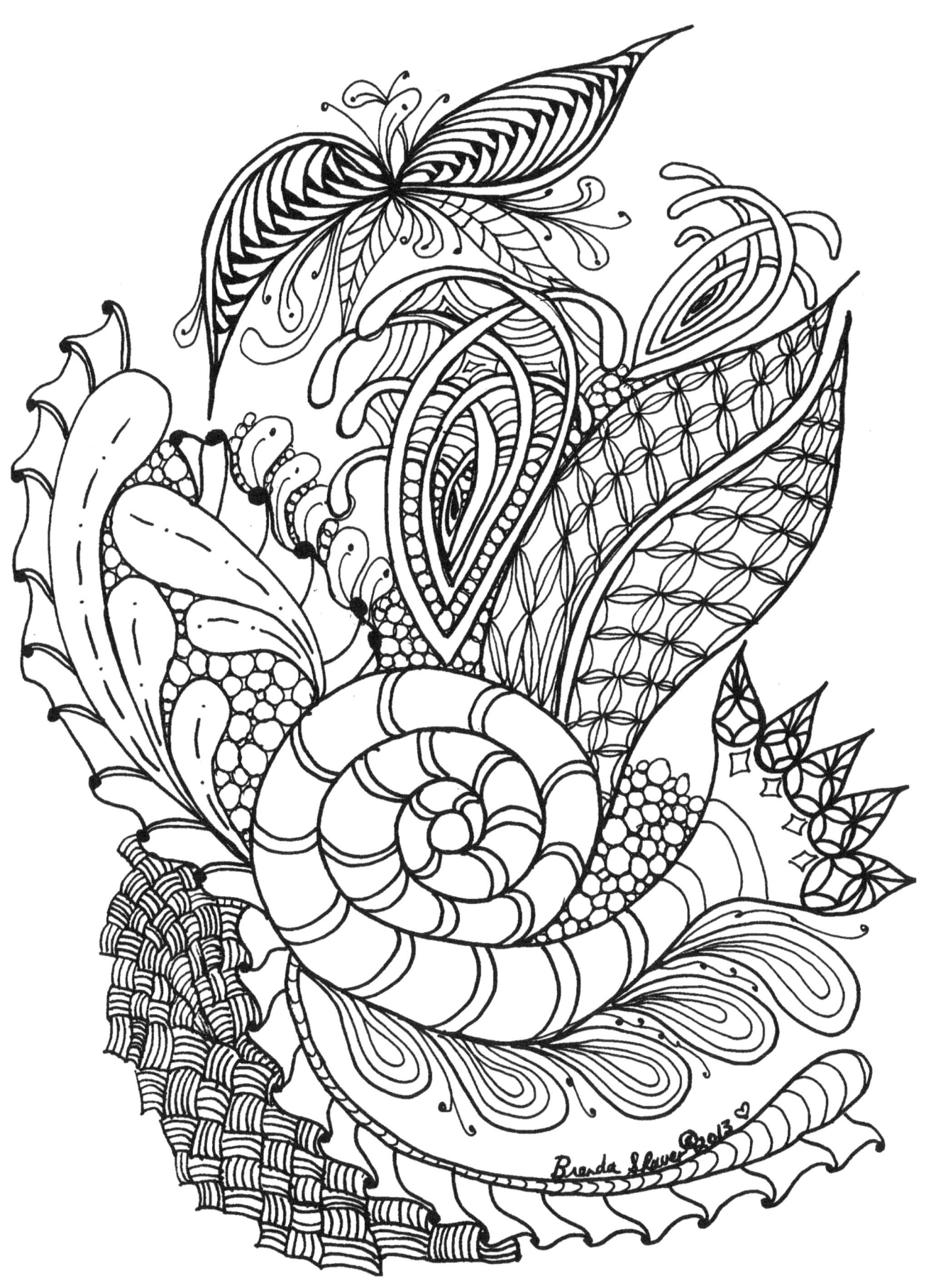
Brenda Shaver 2013

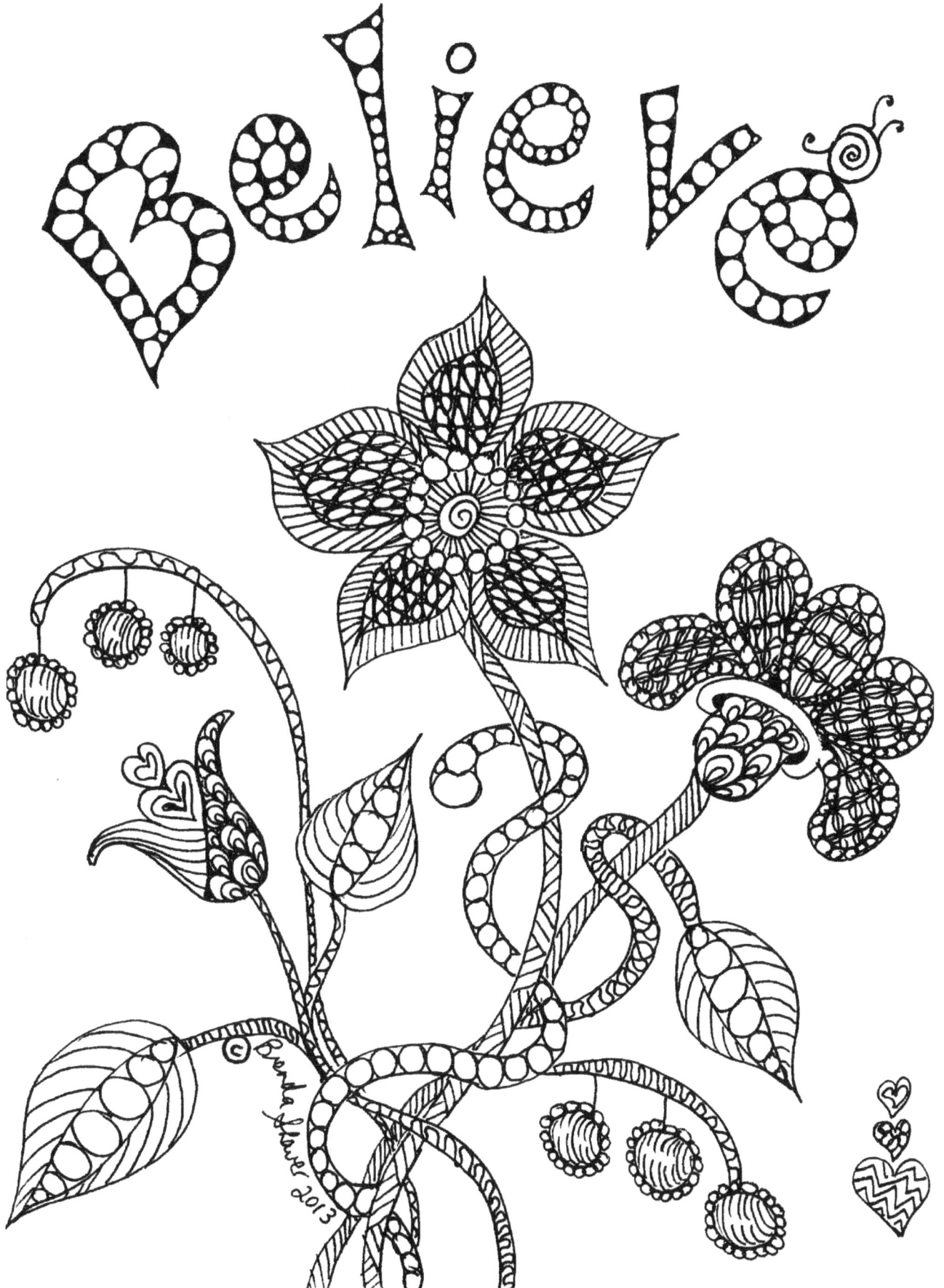

About the Authors

Brenda Shaver: Lifelong arts and crafts entrepreneur who found her true calling as an instructor in the Zentangle® Method in 2012. Brenda wholly embraced Zentangle as the art form for everyone who appreciates beauty in shapes and colors. Students are from every walk of life and many never imagined they could draw and create beautiful art. Brenda and many of her Zentangle students realize the additional benefits of chronic pain management through the focus and creativity that "tangling" brings. Brenda teaches Zentangle as "creativity at its healthiest for mind and body."

Cecilia Lee: A Zentangle prodigy at eight years old, Cecilia drew her first piece of tangled art at the age of four! Cecilia creates her original art in pastels, watercolors and pencil crayons. Cecilia contributed three pages of art in our book by tangling inside stencil shapes of butterflies, moons, stars and hearts.

Spencer Lee: Two year old Spencer is not far behind his cousin Cecilia. He loves to color, especially anything yellow! Spencer creates his own designs in finger painting. His page in our book was developed as he drew strings in pencil for his proud Grammy to tangle in.

Brenda and her grandchildren Cecilia and Spencer reside in the Toronto area of Southern Ontario in Canada.

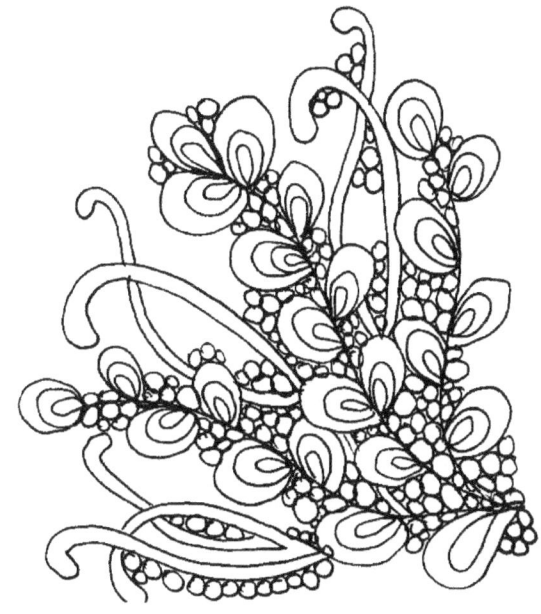